The CHURCH
and the AGE *of*
ENLIGHTENMENT
(1648–1848)

"Dominic A. Aquila has provided a great service to the Church and Catholics in the modern world in this new book. With masterful narrative and insightful focus, Aquila illustrates the military, political, and cultural events of this crucial time period in history. Additionally, he expands the commonly held understanding of the Enlightenment by showing its complexities and the influence of Catholics and the Church during a time of great upheaval that reverberates to the modern day. Aquila's volume is an excellent addition to the outstanding Reclaiming Catholic History series and should be required reading for all students of Catholic history."

Steve Weidenkopf
Author of *The Church and the Middle Ages (1000–1378)*

"Dominic A. Aquila's crisp dissection of the events that followed the Thirty Years' War to the close of the French Revolution reveals the impressive effort of the Catholic Church to challenge the secularizing zeitgeist of the age. In *The Church and the Age of Enlightenment (1648–1815)*, portraits of saints, scholars, painters, warriors, and musicians converge to furnish a fascinating backdrop to the Church's struggle to preserve harmony between faith and reason, and between mind and heart, when myriad forces sought to drive them apart."

Elizabeth Lev
Art historian and instructor at Duquesne University's Italian Campus

"In this excellent book, Dominic A. Aquila introduces us to the world of the Enlightenment, a troubled but brilliant past that has deeply shaped our present age. He captures both its troubles and brilliance, its triumphs and tragedies, through the lives of the most remarkable Catholics of the day. A must read for history buffs who love the Church!"

Christopher T. Baglow
Director of the Science and Religion Initiative at
the McGrath Institute for Church Life
University of Notre Dame

The CHURCH *and the* AGE *of* ENLIGHTENMENT

(1648–1848)

Faith, Science, and the Challenge of Secularism

DOMINIC A. AQUILA

Series Editor, Mike Aquilina

AVE MARIA PRESS AVE Notre Dame, Indiana

⫸ RECLAIMING CATHOLIC HISTORY ⫷

The history of the Catholic Church is often clouded by myth, misinformation, and missing pieces. Today there is a renewed interest in recovering the true history of the Church, correcting the record in the wake of centuries of half-truths and noble lies. Books in the Reclaiming Catholic History series, edited by Mike Aquilina and written by leading authors and historians, bring Church history to life, debunking the myths one era at a time.

The Early Church
The Church and the Roman Empire
The Church and the Dark Ages
The Church and the Middle Ages
The Church and the Age of Reformations
The Church and the Age of Enlightenment
The Church and the Modern Era

For resources to go along with this book, go to https://www.avemariapress.com/church-and-the-age-of-enlightenment-art, or use the following QR code to access the webpage:

Unless otherwise noted, scripture excerpts are from *The Jerusalem Bible*, copyright © 1966 by Darton, Longman & Todd, Ltd. and Doubleday & Company, Inc., a division of Bantam Doubleday Dell Publishing Group, Inc. Used with permission of the publisher.

Series introduction © 2019 by Mike Aquilina

Founded in 1865, Ave Maria Press is a ministry of the United States Province of Holy Cross.

www.avemariapress.com

Paperback: ISBN-13 978-1-64680-031-5

E-book: ISBN-13 978-1-64680-032-2

Cover images © Getty Images.

Cover and text design by Andy Wagoner.

Printed and bound in the United States of America.

Library of Congress Cataloging-in-Publication Data is available.

Contents

⊫ RECLAIMING CATHOLIC HISTORY ⊨
Series Introduction

"History is bunk," said the inventor Henry Ford. And he's not the only cynic to venture judgment. As long as people have been fighting wars and writing books, critics have been there to grumble because "history is what's written by the winners."

Since history has so often been corrupted by political motives, historians in recent centuries have labored to "purify" history and make it a bare science. From now on, they declared, history should record only facts, without any personal interpretation, without moralizing, and without favoring any perspective at all.

It sounds like a good idea. We all want to know the facts. The problem is that it's just not possible. We cannot record history the way we tabulate results of a laboratory experiment. Why not? Because we cannot possibly record all the factors that influence a single person's actions—his genetic makeup, the personalities of his parents, the circumstances of his upbringing, the climate in his native land, the state of the economy, the anxieties of his neighbors, the popular superstitions of his time, his chronic indigestion, the weather on a particular day, the secret longings of his heart.

For any action taken in history, there is simply too much material to record, and there is so much more we do not know and can never know. Even if we were to collect data scrupulously and voluminously, we would still need to assign it relative importance. After all, was the climate more important than his genetic makeup?

But once you begin to select certain facts and leave others out—and once you begin to emphasize some details over others—you have begun to impose your own perspective, your interpretation, and your idea of the story.

Still, there is no other way to practice history honestly. When we read, or teach, or write history, we are discerning a story line. We are saying that certain events are directly related to other events. We say that events proceed in a particular manner until they reach a particular end, and that they resolve themselves in a particular way.

Every historian has to find the principle that makes sense of those events. Some choose economics, saying that all human decisions are based on the poverty or prosperity of nations and neighborhoods, the comfort or needs of a given person or population. Other historians see history as a succession of wars and diplomatic maneuvers. But if you see history this way, you are not practicing a pure science. You are using an interpretive key that you've chosen from many possibilities, but which is no less arbitrary than the one chosen in olden days, when the victors wrote the history. If you choose wars or economics, you are admitting a certain belief: that what matters most is power, wealth, and pleasure in this world. In doing so, you must assign a lesser role, for example, to the arts, to family life, and to religion.

But if there is a God—and most people believe there is—then God's view of things should not be merely incidental or personal. God's outlook should define objectivity. God's view should provide the objective meaning of history.

So how do we get God's view of history? Who can scale the heavens to bring God down? We can't, of course. But since God chose to come down and reveal himself and his purposes to us, we might be able to find what the Greek historians and philosophers despaired of ever finding—that is, the basis for a universal history.

The pagans knew that they could not have a science without universal principles. But universal principles were elusive because no one could transcend his own culture—and no one dared to question the rightness of the regime.

Not until the Bible do we encounter histories written by historical losers. God's people were regularly defeated, enslaved, oppressed, occupied, and exiled. Yet they told their story honestly, because they held themselves—and their historians—to a higher judgment, higher even than the king or the forces of the market. They looked at history in terms of God's judgment, blessings, curses, and mercy. This became their principle of selection and interpretation of events. It didn't matter so much whether the story flattered the king or the victorious armies.

The Bible's human authors saw history in terms of covenant. In the ancient world, a covenant was the sacred and legal way that people created a family bond. Marriage was a covenant, and adoption was a covenant. And God's relationship with his people was always based on a covenant.

God's plan for the kingdom of heaven uses the kingdoms of earth. And these kingdoms are engaged by God and evangelized for his purpose. Providence harnesses the road system and the political system of the Roman Empire, and puts it all to use to advance the Gospel. Yet Rome, too, came in for divine judgment. If God did not spare the holy city of Jerusalem, then neither would Rome be exempted.

And so the pattern continued through all the subsequent thousands of years—through the rise and fall of the Byzantine Empire, the European empires, and into the new world order that exists for our own fleeting moment.

There's a danger, of course, in trying to discern God's perspective. We run the risk of moralizing, presuming too much, or playing the prophet. There's always a danger, too, of identifying God with one "side" or another in a given war or rivalry. Christian history, at its best, transcends these problems. We can recognize that even when pagan Persia was the most vehement enemy of Christian Byzantium, the tiny Christian minority in Persia was practicing the most pure and refined Christianity the world has seen. When God uses imperial structures to advance the Gospel, the imperial structures have no monopoly on God.

It takes a subtle, discerning, and modest hand to write truly Christian history. In studying world events, a Christian historian must strive to see God's fatherly plan for the whole human race and how it has unfolded since the first Pentecost.

Christian history tells the story not of an empire, nor of a culture, but of a family. And it is a story, not a scientific treatise. In many languages, the connection is clear. In Spanish, Portuguese, Italian, and German, for example, the same word is used for "history" as for "story": *historia, história, storia, Geschichte*. In English we can lose sight of this and teach history as a succession of dates to be memorized and maps to be drawn. The timelines and atlases are certainly important, but they don't communicate to ordinary people why they should want to read history. Jacques Barzun complained, almost a half century ago, that history had fallen out of usefulness for ordinary people and was little read. It had fragmented into overspecialized microdisciplines, with off-putting names like "psychohistory" and "quantohistory."

The authors in this series strive to communicate history in a way that's accessible and even entertaining. They see history as true stories well told. They don't fear humor or pathos as threats to their trustworthiness. They are unabashed about their chosen perspective, but they are neither producing propaganda nor trashing tradition. The sins and errors of Christians (even Christian saints) are an important part of the grand narrative.

The Catholic Church's story is our inheritance, our legacy, our pride and joy, and our cautionary tale. We ignore the past at our peril. We cannot see the present clearly without a deep sense of Christian history.

Mike Aquilina
Reclaiming Catholic History Series Editor

Chronology of *The Church and the Age of Enlightenment (1648–1848)*

1602	The Dutch East India Company is founded by the Dutch
1607	The English create a settlement at Jamestown, Virginia
1608	Protestant League of Evangelical Union forms in Europe due to worries about the Habsburgs' influence
1609	Catholic league forms in opposition to the League of Evangelical Union
1615	Dutch found their first colony in North America
1618	The infamous Defenestration of Prague sets off the Thirty Years' War
1618–1625	Bohemian phase of the Thirty Years' War
1624–1642	Reign of the famously hated Cardinal Richelieu
1625–1629	Danish phase of the Thirty Years' War
1629	Edict of Restitution decrees that all lands seized from the Catholic Church since 1552 had to be returned to the Church
1630–1635	Swedish phase of the Thirty Years' War, during which the bubonic plague begins spreading throughout Germany
1634	First Oberammergau Passion Play in response to the plague
1635–1648	French phase of the Thirty Years' War
1639	St. Marie of the Incarnation founds an Ursuline monastery in Quebec, the first institution of learning for women in North America

1644–1648   The Westphalia Conferences, which end in the Peace of Westphalia and the end of the Thirty Years' War

1644–1655   Reign of Pope Innocent X

1649   King Charles I is publicly executed

1650   René Descartes, one of the fathers of the Enlightenment, dies in Stockholm

1651   Publication of Hobbes's infamous book *Leviathan*

1654   Pascal's conversion to Catholicism and "night of fire"

1655   Conversion of Queen Christina of Sweden to Catholicism

1667   Locke's *A Letter Concerning Toleration* is published

1668   Giambattista Vico is born in Naples, Italy

1673   St. Margaret Mary Alacoque's vision of the Sacred Heart of Jesus founds one of the most significant Catholic devotions of all time

1682   Publication of Pierre Bayle's *Diverse Thoughts on Halley's Comet*

1685   Johann Sebastian Bach is born

1687   Condemnation of Quietism by Pope Innocent XI; Newton's *Philosophiae Naturalis Principia Mathematica* is published

1696   St. Alphonsus Liguori is born in Naples, Italy

1699   Locke's *Second Treatise of Government* is published

1706   Mme. Émilie du Châtelet, translator of Newton and key figure in the French tradition of intellectual salons, is born in Paris

1724   Immanuel Kant is born in Königsberg

1738   Freemasonry is first condemned as a heresy

1740	Battista's *The Virgin Appearing to St. Philip Neri* is painted
1741	Handel's composition of *Messiah*
1751	The Academy and College of Philadelphia, which later became the University of Pennsylvania, is founded
1751–1772	Diderot's *Encyclopédie*, one of the first manuals of its kind, is published
1756	Wolfgang Amadeus Mozart is born
1760–1820	Reign of King George III, during which the American Revolution occurred
1762	Rousseau's *Social Contract* is published
1763	Defeat of France in the French and Indian War
1755–1776	Paine's *Common Sense* is published and is circulated (to this day) more widely than any other book in America
1765	The Stamp Act of 1765 infuriates American citizens Mme. Émilie du Châtelet's translation of Newton's *Principia* is published
1770	Raynal's *History of the Two Indias* published Ludwig van Beethoven is born
1773	The Boston Tea Party increases tensions between the Americans and the British
1776	Declaration of Independence *The Wealth of Nations* by Adam Smith is published
1780–1790	Joseph II's decade of reform gives Joseph Eybel an opportunity to argue for Reform Catholicism
1783	American independence is officially recognized by the British

1789   Beginning of the French Revolution, followed by abolition of French feudalism and the writing of the Declaration of the Rights of Man and of the Citizen

1793   Beginning of the Reign of Terror in France

1794   Martyrdom of the sixteen Carmelite sisters and, a while later, the execution of Robespierre

1795   New French Constitution is drafted and approved

1799   Napoleon's coup leads to him declaring himself France's "first consul"; the Napoleonic Era begins

1800   End of French Revolution

1801   John Henry Newman is born in London

1815   End of the Napoleonic Era and Napoleon's exile to St. Helena island

1832   June Uprising in France

1845   John Henry Newman is received into the Roman Catholic Church

1848   Revolutions sweep across continental Europe

1861   Posthumous publication of Jean-Pierre de Caussade's *Self-Abandonment to Divine Providence*

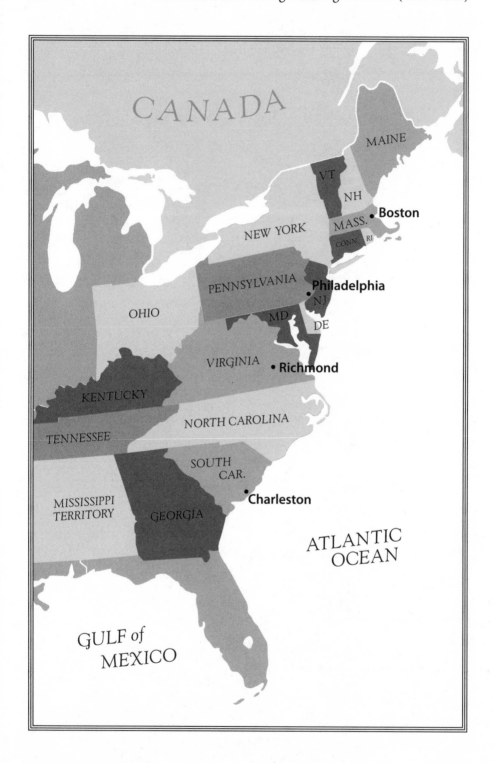

Map xix

Introduction

This book is the story of the Enlightenment era of Western civiliza-tion, set between the years 1648 and 1848. It outlines the main intellec-tual, religious, political, and cultural themes of the period, with special attention to what is often overlooked in other histories of the Enlighten-ment. A particular focus of the story is the place of the Catholic Church and rank-and-file Catholics during this period. Many accounts of the Enlightenment ignore or discount the highly significant contributions of Catholic religious and laity to science, the arts, and the betterment of human life. In fact, it is not unusual for mainstream histories of the Enlightenment to cast unfairly the Catholic Church as hostile to the advance of knowledge and the well-being of society. Relying on primary and secondary historical sources, this book revises this incomplete and unbalanced narrative. It also includes key works of visual art and music from the period, which can be found at https://www.avemariapress.com/church-and-the-age-of-enlightenment-art. Their inclusion is not inci-dental but rather integral to understanding the period, insofar as the arts are reflective of the period in which they were created and, in turn, influence historical developments.

As with any era, dating the Enlightenment is a convention among historians, useful for the coherent discussion of its main ideas and events. This book dates the Enlightenment between 1648 and 1800, two import-ant years for the Church and Western civilization. The former year marks the end of the Thirty Years' War, a bitterly fought and highly destruc-tive European civil war; the latter, a year that marked the end of the French Revolution, which realized the principles of the Enlightenment and changed the world forever. The final chapter of this book covers briefly the aftermath and reactions to the Enlightenment, bringing the story up to the year 1848. These major political and social events bookend an era marked by upheavals in thought, religious commitments, social relations, education, and culture with consequences reaching into the twenty-first century.

Of central importance to the Enlightenment project was undoing the authority of tradition and particularly the time-tested fusion of classical learning and Christian thought that had guided the development of Western civilization. Emboldened by the power of scientific reasoning for mastering nature and organizing human society, European and American men and women of influence tended to devalue or dismiss received ways of thinking. John Locke's (1632–1704) *tabula rasa*—his belief that a person comes into the world as a blank slate—also characterizes the way many Enlightenment influencers thought about the societies they inherited. What came before them was mostly irrelevant, unreliable, or unnecessary in shaping an enlightened human society and rewriting the possibilities of human life. The expansion of educational opportunities and new media enabled by the printing press dramatically enlarged the size of a literate public receptive to new thinking. This conceptual transformation—associated most clearly with what we now call the scientific revolution, extended to areas of nature and human activity beyond the imagination of most pre-Enlightenment thinkers. By the end of the eighteenth century, the stature of pre-Enlightenment thought and institutions had declined sharply. Educated Europeans and Americans believed that with their new ways of knowing they could come to master the world aright for the first time in human history.

As an institution of long-standing importance and influence in shaping pre-Enlightenment European society, the Catholic Church became an object of suspicion and derision to those committed to the Enlightenment program. Many rejected the Church's 1,500-year role in the development of disciplined thinking, systematic education, science, and care for the well-being of persons and society. Like the thought leaders living in the Enlightenment era period, mainstream historians of the twentieth and twenty-first century looking back to the Enlightenment also tend to overlook the Church's crucial pre-Enlightenment contributions to human thought, society, and culture.

But even more regrettable, the current historical narrative of the Enlightenment continues to ignore the innumerable contributions of Catholic religious and laity to the Enlightenment project in mathematics, astronomy, chemistry, biology, physics, geography, navigation, the arts, and human improvement. Among them are Blaise Pascal (1623–1662), a preeminent mathematician, physicist, inventor, writer, and philosopher; Maria Gaetana Agnesi (1718–1799), an accomplished mathematician who wrote on differential and integral calculus; Laura Bassi (1711–1778), a physicist at the University of Bologna and the first woman to be offered a professorship at a European university; and Fr. Václav Prokop Diviš (1698–1765), a physicist who studied electrical phenomena and, among other inventions, constructed the first electrified musical instrument in history. In the Americas, Eusebio Kino (1645–1711), a Jesuit missionary, mathematician, astronomer, and cartographer, mapped California, proving that it was not an island, as his contemporaries thought. He published an astronomical treatise in Mexico City of his observations of the Kirch comet and provided detailed accounts of the origins and progress of the California Missions.

A chief characteristic of the Enlightenment is its elevation of human reason to near mystical heights. It rejected the historic understanding of faith as human participation in divine knowledge and ranked ideas and systems of idea (ideologies) above the mind's openness to the fullness of reality. In doing so, it ignored the wisdom of the Christian tradition, namely, that reality and human existence cannot be comprehended by abstract reasoning alone, which was the position of many influential Enlightenment writers. The great synthesis of faith and reason achieved by the Church and its many saints insists that reason must take in the totality of reality. When it is faithful to its nature, reason admits the existence of something unseen underpinning what is seen—"the assurance of things hoped for, the conviction of things not seen" (Heb 11:1, Revised Standard Version, Catholic Edition).

Chapter 1

The Thirty Years' War and Its Aftermath

Flung from the High Castle

The Thirty Years' War was a sign of the end times for those who lived through it. Brutality and utter riot upended the foundations of civilized European society. A reign of near continuous violence terrorized the peasantry, villagers, and city dwellers. Soldiers took their compensation by pillaging the property of friend and foe alike. To civilians it didn't matter which army was coming through their locale—Protestant or Catholic, German or Swede, French or Spanish—all lives were endangered.

It all began with a minor diplomatic incident. By 1618, the Protestant Revolt and the Catholic Reformation were a century old. Their positions had hardened. Tensions between Protestants and Catholic remained high throughout the 1500s. The lands along the Rhine River in Central Europe and southern Germany remained predominantly Catholic. Lutherans were the majority in northern Germany, and Calvinists dominated in west-central Germany, Switzerland, and the Netherlands.

To truly understand the religious controversies of the sixteenth and seventeenth centuries, we have to suspend our own twenty-first-century ideas and judgments about religious toleration. Our ethic of toleration developed in part as a consequence of the bloodletting of the Thirty Years'

1

War. In fact, toleration in early seventeenth-century Germany was a pre-scription not for peace but for war. The rulers of every state felt entitled and even required to forbid the practice of more than one religion. For error in doctrine had no rights. Each Protestant ruler in Germany out-lawed the Mass in his domain. Catholic rulers for their part believed that by allowing Protestant practices, they were in effect creating centers of rebellion within their borders.

Germany was ground zero for the war. Unlike today, Germany was not a unified nation but rather a loose assembly of cities and territories. Most Germans were loyal to the long line of Holy Roman Emperors who ruled them since the 1200s. They were in the eyes of the Catholic Church legitimate successors of the Roman Empire. For centuries with little inter-ruption, the emperor was also the king of Germany.[1] In the 1400s, the Habsburg dynasty took over the line of emperors.

The ambitions of the Habsburgs had always unsettled the great powers of Europe—the Netherlands, Denmark, Sweden, Italy, England, and espe-cially France. Lutherans and Calvinists within the empire also worried about the Habsburgs. So much so that in 1608 they formed a Protestant alliance within the staunchly Catholic Holy Roman Empire. The members of this alliance, which they called the League of Evangelical Union, pro-fessed continued allegiance to the emperor. But they complained about his seeming unwillingness to protect their hard-won, centuries-old freedoms from the increasing violent upheavals within the empire. A year following the establishment of the Protestant league, a group of German Catholic princes formed the Catholic league. Like the Protestants, the Catholics publicly supported the emperor but worried that continued civil unrest would destroy the empire from within. Of course, each league blamed the other for causing public strife.

In April 1617, the Holy Roman Emperor Matthias (reigned 1612–1619) ordered both leagues to disband. The Catholics complied; the Protestants refused the order. Matthias then sent two representatives to Prague to open negotiations with the Protestant league. Their mission was to hear and address Protestant grievances. The imperial counselors met with leaders of the Protestant league in Prague Castle, which was the time-honored seat of power for the kings of Bohemia, Holy Roman Emperors, and, in modern times, presidents of Czechoslovakia.

Tempers flared during the talks. A mob of Protestant protesters outside the castle stormed in with the intention of executing the emperor's men by the ancient practice of defenestration—a technical term meaning literally to throw someone out of a window. The two imperial envoys fought heroically for their lives against the crowd. They cried out appeals to the Blessed Virgin Mary for assistance. But their attackers succeeded in forcing them out a high window. Leaning over the windowsill as the two men fell, the leaders of the mob taunted them: "We will see if your Mary can help you!"[2] Apparently, she did.

The "Defenestration of Prague" stands as one of the most famous diplomatic incidents in history. Amazingly, the emperor's representatives survived the fall. What then unfolded was a series of diplomatic reactions accompanied by an increasingly heated propaganda war. The emperor and his supporters interpreted the survival of the representatives as a sign that their cause was just. Divine power, through Mother Mary's intercession, had intervened to save them. Protestants dismissed this reading of the event. The representatives were saved because they had fallen into a pile of manure that had been lying by the castle walls. No divine intervention was involved in the matter.

The incident and the war of words around it enflamed both sides and went from words to arms. Eventually, the conflict became international in scope, drawing in more than twenty nations by its end. Those living at the time were overwhelmed by the unprecedented scale of the Thirty Years' War. They referred to it as the Great War, a descriptor that persisted until the First World War of the twentieth century took over the title, thus suppressing the searing memory of the Thirty Years' War.

But for European thought leaders living in the tumultuous aftermath of the Thirty Years' War, the war was the logical outcome of dynastic tribalism and religious differences. To the "enlightened" elite of the seventeenth and eighteenth centuries, the differences that led to the war were little more than outmoded superstitious squabbles or nationalist prejudices. Did not humankind share a common nature? Was not the natural world ordered and ruled by unchanging laws discoverable by the power of human reason alone? Was not then adherence to human reason superior to mental outlooks tainted by ethnic, nationalist, and sectarian loyalties? For those who answered these questions in the affirmative, the Christian religion that had so bitterly divided Europe had to be subordinated to the rule of universal, secular reason. The suppression of Christianity was their prime directive, superseding even the secondary problem of national and dynastic discord.

Ideas Whose Time Had Come

Ideas have consequences. This saying is true for any period in history, but especially so for the Enlightenment. The tumult of the Thirty Years' War created the social conditions for Enlightenment ideas to set in motion far-reaching and momentous changes in Europe and eventually the world. They transformed the way Europeans thought about human nature and the universe. The thought leaders of the Enlightenment trumpeted a "new philosophy" that challenged traditional religious beliefs about miracles, divine revelation, the authority of the Churches (Catholic and Protestant), virtue, and vice. They brought forward new ideas about government, society, and nature. They viewed with suspicion all traditional ways of thinking and all traditional authority. In short, the Enlightenment project started a cultural transformation more revolutionary than anything that had yet occurred in the history of the human race.

The seeds of the Enlightenment revolution had been planted in the 1500s. But they did not flourish until the mid-1600s. The revolution began with the age-old human fascination with the sky. Nicolaus Copernicus (1473–1543), a priest and highly accomplished physician, mathematician, and astronomer, proposed that the sun and not the Earth was the center of the universe. In doing so, he called into question a view of the cosmos that had held sway for well over a thousand years. Copernicus did not mean to stir controversy with his proposal. There was not a whiff of ambition about him. In fact, he refused to publish his heliocentric theory without solid proof that it was true.

There are those today who believe that the Catholic Church is an enemy of science. But it was prominent Catholic churchmen who enthusiastically encouraged Copernicus to publish his theory. He eventually did so, dedicating his groundbreaking book, *On the Revolutions of the Heavenly Spheres* (1543), to Pope Paul III, who willingly accepted the dedication. The Church's encouragement for Copernicus—today regarded as the father of astronomy—was part of its centuries-long patronage of science. In fact, no other institution in history has a longer track record of benevolent support for scientific inquiry than the Catholic Church.[3]

Like Copernicus, Galileo Galilei (1564–1642) insisted that theories had to prove their worth with hard evidence. But he needed technology to acquire the proof needed to validate Copernicus's theory. Galileo had heard about the efforts of a German-Dutch glassmaker to grind lenses that would aid the human eye in viewing distant objects in space. Galileo secured this new technology and improved it. The result was a telescope of unprecedented magnifying power. Turned up to the night sky, Galileo's telescope enabled him to observe the movements of the planets and prove the truth of Copernicus's theory.

Careful observation of the world was the cornerstone of Galileo's method. Francis Bacon (1561–1626), another key figure of the early Enlightenment, also emphasized the importance of observation. It was for him the basis of knowledge. He established it as the first principle of a new kind of science. More so than any other Enlightenment thinker, Bacon was extremely disdainful of traditional ways of reasoning about nature. For they relied more on books and debates among scholars than on the study of nature. He called for a great renewal in how humans acquired and used knowledge. In his view, the learning of the past was barren. It provided little benefit to people's everyday lives. Bacon viewed knowledge as an untapped power for subduing nature for the benefit of humanity. If knowledge did not materially improve people's lives, it was worthless. Human progress, argued Bacon, depended on the widespread use of his new system of inductive, experimental reasoning.

Copernicus, Galileo, and Bacon were just three of the many brilliant figures who laid the groundwork for the full-blown expansion of the Enlightenment in the latter part of the seventeenth century. It took a major upheaval in European society to create the social and cultural conditions for the new ideas of the Enlightenment to gain acceptance. That upheaval was the Thirty Years' War. Waged in stages between 1618 and 1648, it was a cataclysmic civil war fought over complicated, explosive, and contradictory religious and political differences.

There is no denying that before and during the war, Enlightenment thinkers found an audience for their new ideas. New inventions, such as the printing press, the expansion of educational opportunities, and the rise of an educated, reading public, helped circulate their writings. But the Enlightenment's accelerant was the war and its aftermath. Thirty years of intermittent warfare tore apart the fabric of European society. The war's savagery, famine, and disease were commonplace throughout Central Europe. The war wiped out almost a third of Germany's population. The prewar institutions that gave people their bearings and the beliefs that ordered their lives lay in tatters. Postwar conditions were highly favorable to new ways of thinking and doing things. The time had come to try out the new ideas of the Enlightenment.

The Four Phases of the Thirty Years' War

The defenestration incident at Prague Castle sparked the first of four phases of the Thirty Years' War: the Bohemian phase (1618–1625), after which followed the Danish phase (1625–1629), the Swedish phase (1630–1635), and the French phase (1635–1648).

The Bohemian phase began soon after the death of Emperor Matthias in 1619. His successor, Ferdinand II of the House of Habsburg (reigned 1619–1637), was less inclined than Matthias to pursue a diplomatic solution to the religious and political conflicts within the empire. He threatened to use military force to break up the Protestant league. The league responded to the emperor's threats by refusing to acknowledge Ferdinand II's title to the throne of Bohemia, which all previous emperors had held. Instead, they elected a Calvinist king, Frederick V, called the "Winter King" because of his short reign. Frederick's election prompted a massive invasion of imperial forces led by Field Marshal Johann Tserclaes, count of Tilly. The embattled Protestant league appealed to other Protestant rulers and communities across Europe for support with little result.

Count Tilly's armies handily won a series of demoralizing victories against the Protestants. Tilly had subdued the rebellion. Its leaders were executed; their property, confiscated. But the rout of the Protestant forces had an unintended consequence. Tilly's success intensified the concern of other nations—Catholic and Protestant—about Habsburg ambitions and power. To them, the emperor's success in the Bohemian phase of the war signaled a consolidation and expansion that threatened the balance of power among European nations.

The second phase of the war, the Danish phase, expanded the war zone beyond Bohemia. European powers' growing uncertainty over imperial territorial interests moved Denmark's King Christian IV, a Lutheran, to invade Central Europe in 1625. The French backed the Danes' move with financial support, but not troops.

The Danish campaign against the Holy Roman Empire was disastrous. Imperial armies led by the strange but formidable Albrecht von Wallenstein turned back King Christian's invasion and brought the fight to the Danish homeland. In defeat, Denmark settled on terms dictated by the emperor at the Treaty of Lübeck in northern Germany in 1629.

Although the Danish phase of the war was a total victory for the empire, Wallenstein's invasion of Denmark and the brutality of his mercenary armies horrified Europeans. The Swedes perceived his surge northward to the Baltic Sea as a clear threat to their dominion over the Baltic Sea. It seemed to Sweden and other European nations that the Holy Roman Empire was not only consolidating power within Central Europe but also expanding it to northern Europe. There was also clear evidence that Emperor Ferdinand II was meddling in Sweden's internal affairs in an attempt to undermine the legitimacy of Sweden's monarch, King Gustavus Adolphus—"the Lion of the North."

The success against the Danes fortified Emperor Ferdinand's confidence, which he underscored with the Edict of Restitution (1629). The edict rolled back much of the gains of the sixteenth-century Protestant revolt. It decreed that all lands seized from the Catholic Church since 1552 had to be returned to the Church. Surprisingly, France's reaction to the edict put the interest of the French state over its loyalty to the interests of the Catholic Church. Together with Europe's Protestant nation, France launched a propaganda campaign against the emperor in the name of safeguarding German liberties. The man who coordinated the campaign was Cardinal Richelieu (1585–1642), France's de facto prime minister under King Louis XIII.

The third phase of the war began when Sweden invaded Central Europe in 1630. With financial support from France, King Adolphus landed a well-trained, well-armed force on an island off the northeast coast of Germany. In a series of brilliantly led campaigns, the Swedish army managed to push the imperial forces well into southern Germany.

Adolphus's war aims were to restore Protestant rights in Germany and establish a Protestant federation throughout north-central Europe under Swedish patronage. This turn of events in the war, which now positioned Sweden as a new Central European power, alarmed the French. In a fascinating twist, the Swedes and the French who had made common cause against the Holy Roman Empire, now found themselves working at cross-purposes.

The remarkable military successes of the Swedes owed much to the leadership of Gustavus Adolphus and to the absence of Wallenstein as leader of the imperial armies. Emperor Ferdinand had fired Wallenstein because he was too unpredictable and difficult to control. In 1632, with Sweden notching victory after victory, Ferdinand reinstated Wallenstein. Wallenstein contained the Swedish advance and forced the Swedes to join battle at Lützen, a town just southwest of Leipzig. King Adolphus was mortally wounded in the battle, which greatly demoralized the Swedish army. Nevertheless, the Swedes managed to hold their own in the field for a while against Wallenstein's superior forces. But eventually Wallenstein's armies pushed them back across the Baltic Sea. Soon after, in 1634, Wallenstein met his end at the hands of imperial assassins who feared his dictatorial ambitions.

The defeat of the Swedes opened the fourth and decisive French phase in 1635. It lasted thirteen years and marked a departure from the way Cardinal Richelieu sought to manage French involvement in the war. He had been supporting the enemies of the emperor with money, propaganda, and diplomatic maneuvers but avoided committing French troops to the war. But with the defeat of the Danes and the Swedes, Richelieu felt compelled to commit French troops to the war. He opened a two-front war: Germany to the east and Habsburg Spain to the west. The French intervention against Catholic states, even though the French ruling class was Catholic, is a perfect example of Richelieu's doctrine of raison d'état, "reason of state." It meant that the interests of the French monarchy were more important than religious consistency.

French forces fought against Spain successfully, scoring a significant victory at Rocroi in 1643. They also moved decisively into southern Germany. The new Holy Roman Emperor Ferdinand III (reigned 1637–1657) sought an end to the war. Peace talks began in 1643, but the war dragged on till 1848, when all sides to the conflict, exhausted by a constant state of war, signed the Treaty of Westphalia. (For a full-color map illustrating the religious divisions of Central Europe, see illustration 1.1 at https://www.avemariapress.com/church-and-the-age-of-enlightenment-art.)

The Experience of War: Notes from the Field

Dividing the Thirty Years' War into phases based on military campaigns is one important way to understand the war's impact on European society. But to really appreciate the effect of the war on the lives of the people involved, we need a ground-level perspective. Understanding the actions, experiences, sufferings, and perceptions of everyday people helps us see why postwar Europeans were so receptive to the Enlightenment's new ideas about religion and society.

Let's first take a look at life from the perspective of soldiers and civilians. The relationship between them was especially significant because the armies of all sides supplied themselves mostly from what their soldiers stole or extorted from peasants and villagers. But not all civilians were passive victims. Some fought back against the soldiers or deployed other resistance strategies.

The following encounter between Johan, an imperial cavalryman, and Karl, a shepherd is typical. The residents of Ottobeuren in southern Germany were forced to quarter Johan's regiment. Johan went through the countryside in search of food for his men. Not too far from town he met Karl tending a flock of sheep. Johan demanded that Karl provide his men with lambs from his sheepfold. Karl's friends standing within ear-shot overheard the demand and ran to get the town's elderly mayor to intercede with Johan on behalf of Karl. As soon as the mayor appeared, Johan pulled out a pistol and shot him dead. That same night imperial soldiers plundered Karl's village, killing and injuring many of its inhab-itants. In retaliation, Karl and his neighbors ambushed three soldiers on watch outside Ottobeuren. Infuriated by this brazen act, the soldiers of the regiment plundered what was left of Karl's village and continued their rampage through the surrounding countryside. Undeterred, Karl gath-ered a posse and assassinated a high-ranking officer of the imperial army and fled to another town.[4]

Not all conflicts between soldiers and civilians became cycles of vio-lent retribution. Some were settled through what elements of law remained in force. The residents of Dierdorf in western Germany were forced to quarter a regiment of imperial mercenaries. As often would happen, a soldier of the regiment—in this case, Peter Hagendorf—had too much drink and wandered into an area where peasants had organized a resis-tance movement. Three peasants hidden in the brush attacked, robbed, and stripped him. Naked, disheveled, and humiliated, Peter returned to the jeers of his regiment.

Soon after this incident, Peter's regiment joined battles all around the Rhineland. All the while, his companions never lost an opportunity to retell the story of Peter's humiliation at the hands of mere peasants. After several months, the regiment returned to Dierdorf. Peter searched the countryside around Dierdorf in search of his assailants and found one of them walking along the road. Peter brought him before the military police and then to jail, demanding the return of his belongings under penalty of death. The field marshal in command of the area heard Peter's case and, in front of those before whom Peter suffered embarrassment, declared that the peasant should be hung if restitution to Peter was not forthcoming. The authorities of the village came to the peasant's rescue and paid triple the amount stolen from Peter, which Peter then shared in common with his commanding officers.[5]

The chaos and desperation brought on by the Thirty Years' War also brought violence to Catholic institutions, symbols, traditions, and ideals, mostly from Protestant soldiers, but from Catholics as well. In the mid-1630s, for example, the villagers of Andechs in southern Germany had been suffering the terrors of war for more than a decade. The contesting armies of King Gustavus Adolphus of Sweden and Emperor Ferdinand II crisscrossed the neighboring countryside, leaving behind disease, starvation, and the scars of unspeakable violence and brutality. Many had taken refuge with others from nearby towns in the monastery of Heiligenberg. They thought they'd find safety there under the protection of the good abbot Maurus Friesenegger.

But starving soldiers quartered near the monastery took no account of the time-honored tradition of sanctuary. Desperate soldiers confiscated what little provision the villagers had managed to store on the monastery grounds. The monks of the abbey baked bread, and bakers from other nearby towns sent whatever they could to feed the Andechians and the soldiers. The provisions sent from elsewhere fell to robbers, and those carrying them were beaten or murdered. Cut off from their supply lines, soldiers fought with villagers and farmers for what food there was; some resorted to eating dogs, cats, and vermin. Rumors spread that there were even acts of cannibalism in Agawang, near Augsburg.

Chaos and violence had shattered the contemplative calm that Abbot Maurus spent his life protecting. Now, surrounded by suffering on a scale he could not have imagined, he took up the duties of ministering to hundreds for whom death, "that evil about all other evils," was preferable to their current condition. Looking out over villagers and soldiers packed together within the walls of the monastery, he saw jaundiced, sunken faces and emaciated bodies draped in rags. His monks heard the confessions of the dying nonstop, day after day. The dead lay in open fields because graves could not be dug quickly enough. Beyond the monastery walls he heard the constant pounding and hammering of villagers' houses being torn apart to provide firewood for the armies.

Amid this hellish scene, the abbot took in a sight he thought to himself would have been comical had not the circumstances been so dire. A group of hungry infantrymen had heard there were a few pigs left hidden in stalls on the monastery grounds. They broke into the stalls, and in the process the pigs escaped. The officers in charge ran after the soldiers who were in turn chasing after the pigs. Abbot Maurus recorded the scene in his diary: "If, in these times," he wrote, "we had been able to laugh, then this certainly would have been a funny scene to see, with the rank and file chasing the pigs across the field, and the officers chasing the rank and file across the field, all of the scoundrels with their rags flying in the air and the officers with flying hair."[6]

The comic interlude did not last long as Abbot Maurus turned to inspect the monastery's horrifically violated Church. Nothing was sacred anymore. The putrid stench of horse manure and the decaying feed in troughs left on the altar sickened him. His heart sank as he saw offering boxes smashed and the grave of the monastery's founding abbot desecrated by Swedish soldiers. The image of St. Rasso, the great patron of Heiligenberg, which had hung over the high altar, lay on the ground smeared with manure.

Amid this seemingly endless succession of sacrileges, Abbot Maurus witnessed a miracle. A painting of the Blessed Virgin hanging over the high altar was untouched and undamaged. Despite their most strenuous efforts, the soldiers of King Gustavus Adolphus could not dislodge the image of the Mother of God. Frustrated by their fruitless tries, they were certain that behind the painting there must be hidden a treasure of great value. When the soldiers reported their efforts to their commanding officer, he forbade them from laying another hand on the image. The king's army, he said, would not engage in holy war against such a sacred image.

The miraculous preservation of the Virgin's portrait was a sign to Abbot Maurus that the Heiligenberg monastery was under the protection of the Mother of God. For it had not suffered the typical fate of other holy sites in the region. To prevent Catholic worship and pilgrimages, the Swedish army and their Protestant allies had set fire to churches, cathedrals, monasteries, and shrines. Protestants and Catholics alike marveled that Abbot Maurus's monastery was still standing. People throughout the surrounding countryside asked, "What sort of place was Heiligenberg that it was spared the torch?"[7]

Torture was also commonplace. Martin, a Protestant minister in northern German, was captured and tortured by imperial troops in his home city of Heldburg. The imperials had been extorting money and supplies from the occupants of the city, who lived under the constant threat of impending annihilation. When Martin failed to supply his captors with any useful information about other civilians, they tortured him using a method called the Swedish cocktail, a forerunner to modern-day water boarding. It was a technique eventually picked up and used by all European militaries. Twice in one hour, his captors forced manure-laced water down Martin's throat until his distended stomach was ready to explode. The pain was excruciating, and his teeth were jarred loose by the stick his torturers inserted into his mouth. When Martin continued to say nothing of value about his neighbors, the soldiers dragged him out to be hung. He managed to escape his captors and hid under a bridge until, under cover of night, he returned to his family hiding in the outskirts of Heldburg.[8]

Besides the innumerable deaths from war-related violence, hundreds of civilians died of diseases spread by the invading armies. Bubonic plague raged through southern Germany during the Swedish phase of the war. In one instance a man traveling back to the town Oberammergau in Bavaria had unknowingly brought the plague with him. The plague killed the man and began spreading through Oberammergau. The inhabitants of Oberammergau vowed that if God spared them from the plague, in return they would reenact the Passion of Christ every ten years. Following the vow, no other inhabitant of Oberammergau came down with the plague, and supposedly, those infected with it recovered.

The world-famous Oberammergau Passion Play was first performed in 1634. It included more than over two thousand actors, singers, instrumentalists, and production technicians, all residents of the town. Oberammergauians kept their promise, with a few notable exceptions. In 1770, the celebrated Enlightenment ruler Elector Maximilian III, then duke of Bavaria, banned all passion plays, as part of a drive against extravagance. The circumstances of the First and Second World War also prevented the play's performance.[9] More recently, in a curious reminder of the play's origins, the COVID-19 pandemic forced the cancellation of the 2020 performance of the Oberammergau Passion Play.

The Aftermath of the Thirty Years' War

The Thirty Years' War was the last of the wars of religion, the series of skirmishes and wars that had disrupted Europe since the Protestant revolt of the early 1500s. The Peace of Westphalia that brought an end to the Thirty Years' War was the first of the great peace conferences of modern times. No side emerged from the peace conference victorious. The treaty signaled the utter exhaustion of all combatants. Central Europe lay in ruins. Its population was two-thirds of what it was before the war. The Swedes alone razed approximately 2,000 castles, 18,000 villages, and 1,500 towns. Germany splintered into hundreds of mostly ineffective, semi-independent states. The Holy Roman Empire retreated to Austria and the Habsburg lands. The Westphalia accords formalized the Catholic, Lutheran, and Calvinist religious divide in Germany, with people either converting or relocating to areas controlled by rulers of their own faith.

The war's toll was so massive that it evoked impassioned reactions from every social class, but especially from Europe's educated classes, who gained greater influence as sovereigns and other leaders listened more attentively to alternative ways to rule in post-Westphalia Europe. Even though religious motives for the war had given way gradually to political and dynastic ones, the European elites insisted on seeing it mainly as a war of religions. They asked repeatedly in many different forums and publications how any justification could be given for the violence that Christians had wrought upon Christians in the name of faith and salvation.

Up Close and Personal:

ST. VINCENT DE PAUL (1581–1660)

The work of St. Vincent de Paul is synonymous with concern for the poor and the forgotten. Known as "Father of the Poor" and "Apostle of Charity," his followers and the institutions he created were first on the scene in the French regions ravaged by the Thirty Years' War. As the French government was financing the Protestant states in the war, St. Vincent directed war relief efforts in the areas trampled by their armies and the Catholic armies of the Holy Roman Empire. During and after the war, St. Vincent and his Vincentian priests and brothers and the daughters of charity rushed food, clothing, and supplies to the borderlands between France and Germany. They also provided the sacraments and spiritual consolation to those trying to rebuild their lives.

Vincent was deeply troubled by the report from missionaries working in the field. One of his Vincentians, Fr. Julian Guerin, wrote:

> I began as soon as I arrived to distribute alms. I find there is such a large number of poor people here that I cannot give something to each; there are more than three

hundred in very great need. . . . More than a hundred
. . . look like skeletons covered with skin and . . . they
present such a horrible appearance that if Our Lord did
not give me strength, I would not dare to look at them.
Their skin is like black marble . . . their eyes and whole
countenance have a scowling appearance. . . . It is the
most dreadful sight I have ever seen. They hunt about in
the fields for roots which they cook and eat.[10]

Moved by reports such as Fr. Guerin's, St. Vincent asked his
Parisian followers to act in solidarity with those suffering from
unprecedented levels of hunger, sickness, and violence in the
provinces. He wrote, "This is a time to do penance since God
is afflicting his people. Should we not be at the foot of the altar
bewailing their sins? We are obliged to do so. But in addition,
should we not retrench some of our usual food for their relief?"[11]
The Vincentians and their followers in Paris thereafter restricted
their meals to black bread.

The scale of suffering and evils confronting St. Vincent were
staggering. Despite his personal pleas to Cardinal Richelieu
for peace, he knew that affairs of state were out of his control.
He resolved that wherever the forces of destruction did their
work, he would send his messengers to restore life. Against the
destroying armies of kings, he opposed his own armies of priests,
brothers, and daughters of charity to alleviate the miseries of war.
As one Vincentian father suggested, perhaps we ought to place
"Apostle of War Relief" alongside St. Vincent's many other titles.

The Arts as Mirrors of Society

For decades to follow, the war became the subject for artists in all media—
painting, music, theater, and literature. A premier example is the work of

Peter Paul Rubens (1577–1640). An artist and skilled diplomat, Rubens worked tirelessly to bring an end to the war. His unique position as both a master painter and a distinguished diplomat deeply informed one of his most famous paintings, *Consequences of War*. (See illustration 1.2 for an image of *Consequences of War* at https://www.avemariapress.com/church-and-the-age-of-enlightenment-art.) The painting is a riot of symbolic commentary on the Thirty Years' War. Among its most prominent symbols is Mars, the god of war, who dominates the center space of the composition. He lunges forward in full battle armor, trampling on a book and a drawing to symbolize the harm done to human civilization during the war. The figure of Alekto, the ancient personification of uncontrollable rage, holds high a torch as she pulls Mars along his path of destruction. Next to Alekto are monsters depicting disease, famine, and the apocalypse. In the lower right of the painting, Rubens shows a mother holding a child to signify the war's annihilation of all human affection, inflicting damage that will persist for generations.

In music, Heinrich Schütz (1585–1672), Germany's greatest composer before Johann Sebastian Bach, gave expression to the religious conflicts of the war in his hauntingly beautiful sacred work *Saul, Saul, Why Do You Persecute Me?* Its text is simple and repetitive: "Saul, Saul, why do you persecute me? / It will be hard for you to kick against the thorns." The text refers to the dramatic conversion of St. Paul at the height of his persecution of Christians. Listeners during the Thirty Years' War heard Schütz's music as a reference to the religious persecutions of their own time. (Listen to musical excerpt 1.1 at https://www.avemariapress.com/church-and-the-age-of-enlightenment-art: Heinrich Schütz, *Saul, Saul, Why Do You Persecute Me?*)

The war also shaped the worldview of Philipp Jakob Spener (1635–1705), the father of German Pietism, an offshoot of Lutheranism. Pietism ranks as one of the greatest movements in Christianity. Spener did not found a new denomination, yet Pietism's influence was extensive. It was the most powerful formative influence on a towering Enlightenment figure, the philosopher Immanuel Kant (1724–1804). Pietism emphasized the importance of personal experience and religious feeling, and undervalued commitments to orthodox Christian doctrines. It thus set the stage for the eventual separation of faith and reason, which had guided Christian thinking before the Enlightenment. It also laid the groundwork for making religion a private matter with little or no connection to public life.

Politically, in the immediate aftermath of the war, Europeans had to confront serious and grave challenges. They needed a reordering of the continent along new lines and principles, not just to prevent a recurrence of religious violence, but more important, to balance the rising power and ambitions of Europe's individual nations. These challenges invited new ideas about morality, good government, international relations, and the role of the new experimental sciences in society. Thinkers from a variety of backgrounds were at the ready to supply novel ways of thinking about these questions. These ideas are the subject of the following chapter.

YOU BE THE JUDGE:

Was the Thirty Years' War fought over religion or politics?

Trustworthy historical accounts of the Thirty Years' War acknowledge the intertwining of the war's religious and political elements. While not denying the political aspects of the war, some historians argue that the war was fought primarily for religious purposes, with countries being drawn into war to defend either Protestantism or Catholicism. Other historians emphasize the primacy of the combatants' political objectives, wherein each used the war as an opportunity to protect and strengthen his position among the rapidly shifting balance of power among the European great powers and dynasties.

The early sixteenth-century revolt of Martin Luther, John Calvin, Henry VIII, and others against the Roman Catholic Church initiated a century of religious conflict in western Europe. There were efforts to ease this conflict, such as the Peace of Augsburg in 1555, whereby heads of states chose their country's religion: Protestant or Catholic. During the Thirty Years' War combatants renounced or just ignored the terms and the spirit of the Peace of Augsburg.

From 1618 through 1625, the war was mostly a civil war among the German principalities with Protestant German states taking up arms against the Austrian Hapsburgs, their German Catholic allies, and Catholic Spain. To be sure issues of political control were involved in the conflict, but many of these issues centered on religious questions. When Denmark entered the war in 1625, the conflict remained primarily religious.

But with the entrance of Gustavus Adolphus of Sweden into the war in 1630, the motives for fighting began to shift. The Swedes were committed Lutherans intent on defeating their Catholic opponents. In this effort the Swedes benefited from covert financial support from Catholic France, whose chief minister was Cardinal Richelieu. How could this be in a war of Protestants against Catholics? Why would a high official of the Catholic Church support a Protestant combatant?

The answer was political: France feared being surrounded by the Hapsburgs to the east and their dynastic ally to the west in Spain. A Catholic victory in Germany would lead to just such a vulnerable geopolitical position. So the French gave money and some war materiel to the Swedes, and then in 1639 entered the war militarily on the side of the Protestants.

The Peace of Westphalia in 1648 ended the Thirty Years' War. Austria was defeated, and its hopes for control over a Catholic Europe disintegrated. The Peace of Westphalia established the religious and political boundaries for Europe for the next two centuries. But even after the Westphalian peace accords, France continued to press for more territorial gains to the disadvantage of Spain.

Given the intensity of the century-long religious conflicts brought on by the Protestant revolt, it is easy to see the Thirty Years' War as a religious war. But is such a view fair and true to the political realities of seventeenth-century Europe?

Chapter 2

What Is the Enlightenment?

The Sacrament of the Present Moment: The Enlightenment's Spiritual Counterculture

"The whole essence of the spiritual life consists in recognizing the designs of God for us at the present moment." Such, in short, is Fr. Jean-Pierre de Caussade's doctrine of the present moment, which he set forth in a series of spiritual conferences for the Sisters of the Visitation in Nancy, France, during the 1740s. The conferences were eventually published as *Self-Abandonment to Divine Providence* (1861), and instantly joined the canon of Christian spiritual classics.

Caussade (1675–1751) joined the Jesuits in 1693. He taught grammar, physics, and logic at the Jesuit College in Toulouse from 1708 to 1714, after which he devoted himself to giving retreats and missions for men and women religious in France. Caussade was a truly unique figure of the Enlightenment era. He was educated in mathematics and the sciences in Jesuit institutions, which were at that time the best in Europe and the Americas. Indeed, Francis Bacon, a trailblazer among secular Enlightenment leaders and a fierce opponent of the Catholic Church, said of the Jesuits, "They are so good that I wish they were on our side."[1] Another Enlightener commented, "One cannot talk about mathematics in the sixteenth and seventeenth centuries without seeing a Jesuit at every corner."[2]

Caussade was well acquainted with the mainstream of Enlightenment thought and the emerging dominance of mathematics and the experimental sciences over nearly every aspect of life. The times lived in him. But

23

unlike many of his Jesuit confreres, he turned from the public world of learned societies and public debates to probe the mysteries of the interior life. His turn toward interiority was not a reactionary escape to a pre-Enlightenment past. Rather, he sought to bring forward classic Christian spiritual practice into a new era that was suspicious, if not contemptuous, of religiosity. Caussade was especially interested in preserving and energizing the full-bodied meanings and purposes of concepts such as mind, faith, reason, and knowledge, which the Enlightenment was redefining and redirecting. In effect, he poured old wine into new wine skins.

Caussade combined the Carmelite mystical theologies of St. John of the Cross (1542–1591) and St. Teresa of Avila (1515–1582), which drew renewed interest through St. John's canonization in 1726; the Salesian spirituality of the winning and gracious St. Francis de Sales (1567–1622); and the spiritual exercises of his order's founder, St. Ignatius of Loyola (1491–1556). The result was a practical way for all to access the contemplative life and lead a life of holiness. Caussade wrote, "Jesus calls all to perfection. . . . If we knew how to leave God's divine hand free to act."[3]

Central to the doctrine of the present moment was faith, which was routinely caricatured by Enlightenment leaders as childish superstition or irrationality. "Faith is what I preach," said Caussade, realized through self-abandonment to the will of God made manifest in the present moment. "The present moment is always full of infinite treasures," said Caussade. "It contains far more than we have the capacity to hold. Faith is the measure; what you find in the present moment will be according to the measure of your faith."[4]

Caussade taught that the grace to know and embrace God's will does not exist in the past, which is gone, or the future, which is yet to be. It is available fully resplendent in the "now." With great subtleness, de Caussade hinted at the new intellectual and cultural assaults on the Christian faith when he wrote, "The life of faith is nothing but the continual pursuit of God through everything that disguises, disfigures, destroys, and so to say, annihilates Him."[5]

Caussade did not emphasize faith at the expense of reason. On the contrary, he wrote that the mind enables humans to know God and thereby to love him. At the same time, in an indirect critique of the Enlightenment's cult of overgrown reason, he pointed out that too great an emphasis on the powers of reason could be perilous. It is like "a dangerous slave" that can turn on its master. "It can do great harm if it is not kept under control."[6]

The Enlightenment tended to put God at a distance from human affairs, when it bothered at all with his existence. Against this tendency, Caussade underscored God's close and abiding interest in each person. His providential design was not remote but a personal address. Using the language of the Enlightenment's obsession with experimental science, Caussade taught that God instructs the human heart through "experimental knowledge," which is how the humanity of Jesus developed. In Caussade's words,

> That which instructs us is what happens from one moment to another producing in us that experimental science which Jesus Christ Himself willed to acquire before instructing others. In fact, this was the only science in which He could grow, according to the expression of the holy Gospel; because being God there was no degree of speculative science which He did not possess. Therefore, if this experimental science was useful to the word incarnate Himself, to us it is absolutely necessary if we wish to touch the hearts of those whom God sends to us. ... We must listen to God from moment to moment to become learned in the theology of virtue which is entirely practical and experimental.[7]

Caussade's doctrine of the present moment was not without controversy. The controversy surrounding his work exemplified the confused and chaotic state of religious belief and practice during the Enlightenment. The

Enlightenment era saw an explosion of religious reforms following on from the Protestant revolt against the Catholic Church in the early 1500s. The Lutheran protest of 1517 inaugurated a cascade of sectarian spinoffs. The Thirty Years' War, with its entanglements of dynastic and religious aims, reinforced the tribalization of Christian sectarianism. Caussade's teaching was caught up in this torrent of religious dissent. Some of Caussade's superiors, anxious about new expressions of Catholic piety, registered concern that Caussade's idea of abandonment to Divine Providence bore too much similarity to the heresy of Quietism condemned by Pope Innocent XI in 1687.

Quietism advocated the silencing of one's will, especially the will to action, which it held to be an offense to God. Quietists believed that total abandonment to the will of God required self-annihilation, which was necessary for the soul to return to its source, the essence of God. Quietism's practice of abandonment was a self-erasing, fatalistic resignation to a universe inhospitable to the deepest longings of the human heart. Such despairing fatalism was precisely what Caussade's submission to the present moment corrected. He saw that Quietists' fatalism was a reaction to the social chaos left by the Thirty Years' Wars and the new Enlightenment science that spoke of a God who once having set the universe in motion was unavailable to the people in it.

Caussade was emphatic that self-abandonment to Divine Providence had nothing in common with Quietism. "It is useless to imagine methods of self-abandonment from which all personal activity is excluded," wrote Caussade. "When the divine plan prescribes action, holiness for us lies in activity."[8] Moreover, as a countercurrent to the elitist tendencies of the Enlightenment, whereby the learned lauded it over the "unenlightened," Caussade presented a simple method of knowing inspired by the Gospel and open to all: "I confess to thee, O Father, Lord of Heaven and earth, because thou hast hid these things from the wise and prudent, and hast revealed them to little ones. Yea, Father: for so hath it seemed good in thy sight" (Mt 11:25–26).

The Enlightenment: Moderate and Radical

Caussade was a member of the Enlightenment's largest organization of learned men, which had an unrivaled unity of purpose: the Society of Jesus. He was educated to meet the challenges posed by the new science and ideas of the Enlightenment and even taught them as a professor at the Jesuit college in Toulouse in a manner consistent with the Catholic intellectual tradition. Yet after a short stint in the public sphere of Enlightenment controversies and discoveries, he decided to live a more hidden life in which he focused intently on the infinitely mysterious interiority of the human person and his or her relation to God.

In so doing he continued a familiar pattern in the Christian tradition. When public spaces become unfriendly or hostile to the expansion and development of Christian ideals and missionary efforts, men and women, at least for a time, turn their attention to the vastness of the interior life. The premiere example of this pattern is St. Augustine's *Confessions*, the first great exploration of selfhood in Western civilization written between AD 397 and 400 as the Roman Empire unraveled and public order with it. Similarly, a century following the death of St. Augustine as European society continued its descent into disorder, St. Benedict, the son of a Roman nobleman, withdrew from public life to focus on a hidden life of ordered prayer and work, which seeded Western monasticism and the eventual reconstruction of Europe.

What was the character and mentality of Enlightenment culture such that in a less than a century Christianity went from being the center and genius of European culture to living on its edge? In short, what was the Enlightenment? The greatest figure of the Enlightenment, the philosopher Immanuel Kant, asked that very question in 1787. At that point the

Enlightenment had been in full swing for more than a century. Kant characterized those hundred or so years as humanity's long overdue coming of age. The Enlightenment in Kant's reading of it meant that humanity had finally threw off all that had infantilized humankind. He summed up the Enlightenment with the motto *Sapere aude*, "dare to know," which signaled a new independence of mind and thought from the external constraints of church and state.

But besides these external impediments to the independence of mind, Kant also declared independence from all of the person's interior dispositions that infringed upon pure thought, in other words, all the qualities of personhood that make one truly human, such as intuition, emotion, sentiment, faith, and instinct. For as much as societal institutions restrained freedom of thought, so too did these aspects of a person's interior life. At the extreme, the human mind for Kant and his Enlightenment colleagues was a thinking machine independent of any relation to one's body, including one's upbringing, personal history, experiences, emotional and spiritual state, and faith commitments.

As critics of the Enlightenment project then and now pointed out, Kant was naive to assume that the act of thinking could be divorced from all the human realities, external and internal, that shape and influence our ways of thinking. His critics aside, Kant and other champions of the Enlightenment either dismissed or minimized the limitations of reason. Instead, they recast the human mind as an instrument for probing the deep workings of nature and society, not so much to appreciate or marvel at them, but rather to master them for the benefit of human material and moral progress.

The rule of Enlightenment reason was measurement. Only that which could be measured in mathematical terms had value. Mathematics as applied to all aspects of the natural world and human affairs was the means by which Enlightenment leaders thought they could obtain certainty about the universe and the people in it. Certainty became an obsession. Their solemn mantra was "what can we know and know with certainty?" Accordingly, mathematics became the gold standard for what real knowledge should be because its formulas and calculations were thought to be free from human bias and certain and true for all times and places. It was a means to discovering universal truth, which theretofore was the province of the universal Church.

To be sure, this narrowing of human reason as solely a tool for measuring and rational analysis produced significant, practical technological advances in human society. It did in fact make life better for more people. The downside of this mindset occurred when it crowded out all other ways of thinking about the world. If something could not be understood by the Enlightenment's new mode of calculating reason, then it was considered unimportant and moved to the fringes of public life. Decisions affecting the common life of men and women had to be based on certain or near-certain knowledge, such as that which mathematics provided, and certainly not something as imprecise as religious faith. By this movement, religion became a private, personal matter of diminishing importance to the common good of society.

The Enlightenment's isolation of the human mind from all external and internal influences and the reduction of reasoning to mere calculation assaulted the long-cherished dignity of reason and knowledge, and the Christian synthesis of faith and reason. Commenting on the Enlightenment's exaggerated faith in rationalism, Alfred North Whitehead, a prominent twentieth-century mathematician and philosopher, said that while "the Middles Ages were an age of faith based on reason, the 18th century [the age of the Enlightenment], was an age of reason based on faith."[9] For the most enthusiastic among the Enlightenment *philosophes*, the mind alone gave life meaning and value. This distorted view of human reason led the great historian, Christopher Dawson, to view the Enlightenment, especially its French version, as "the last of the great European heresies."[10]

The Philosophes: Thought Leaders of the Enlightenment

The thought leaders of the Enlightenment were primarily philosophers, but few of them held university positions as nearly all philosophers do today. They were what the French called *philosophes*—learned men (and some women) who claimed to bring independent reasoning to religion, science, politics, economics, and the social issues of their time. Besides philosophers, the Enlightenment movement included scientists, historians, political leaders, playwrights, writers, visual artists, and composers from Europe and the Americas. Its greatest centers of influence were England, Scotland, Germany, and France.

Enlightenment thinking about the world and human society nearly always attempted to start from scratch, with a mind uninfluenced by the past, societal institutions, or personal temperaments. The Enlightenment generation was cynical about history. Many of its members viewed history as a catalog of crimes, cruelty, and knavery. At best, history and tradition offered them a mixture of truth and error, with most of the errors stemming from religious beliefs and practices. Given this view of the past and a belief in the autonomy of the human mind, the idea of a *tabula rasa*—a blank slate—had great appeal to Enlighteners, as a way both to think about the education of children and to shape the new society they were midwifing into being.

Isaac Newton: The Father of the Enlightenment

The best way to fully understand the Enlightenment is to study its most significant figures. Chief among them was Sir Isaac Newton (1643–1727), the world's greatest mathematician and physicist, and the very personification of the Enlightenment way of being. If the community of *philosophes* could have canonized one of their own, it would have been him. For Voltaire (1694–1778), a preeminent French Enlightenment philosopher and writer, Newton was the greatest man who ever lived. "We are all his disciples now," wrote Voltaire.[11] The Scottish historian, philosopher, and economist David Hume (1711–1776), in an uncharacteristic burst of praise, wrote, "In Newton, this island [Britain] may boast of having produced the greatest and rarest genius that ever rose for the ornament and instruction of the species."[12]

Newton once said that he had seen farther because he stood on the shoulders of giants. This well-known saying of Newton's seems to credit the great minds of the past and his contemporaries for his world-class achievements. If we took this remark at face value, it would seem to run counter to the Enlightenment distrust of the past and the influence of other minds. But as Newton's most insightful biographer observed, Newton's remark was disingenuous to say the least.[13]

Newton cultivated solitude and isolation obsessively. He fit the cliché of the reclusive and preoccupied genius. He seemed socially odd to those who knew him personally and was given to prolonged periods of self-isolation and excessive suspiciousness. Born into a humble family living in a small English village near Grantham, Lincolnshire, Newton early on demonstrated an intelligence beyond his years. As a boy he tinkered constantly, building windmills, kites, and water clocks. His extraordinary mathematical abilities as a student at Cambridge University earned him a professor's chair when he was just twenty-three years old. Before he turned twenty-six he had invented differential and integral calculus in order to explain the elliptical orbits of the planets.

During the most productive periods of his life he doubled down on his self-isolation. In a stunning contrast to his reputation for hard-boiled rationalism and experimental rigor, his passionate interest was alchemy, a cultish pseudo-science cloaked in secrecy. Newton dreaded the peering eyes of critics, shrank from controversy, and rarely published his findings. Striving to solve the mysteries of the universe, his life mimicked the complex secrecy in which he saw them concealed.

By any standard, Newton's contributions to mathematics and physics were astonishing. But to his Enlightenment disciples what mattered most beyond his particular discoveries and inventions was his single-minded dedication to experimenting. Newton would not back any idea, principle, or theory unless it had been absolutely confirmed by experiments. His motto, *hypotheses non fingo*, "I feign no hypotheses," had a special appeal to his Enlightenment contemporaries. It stood for an unwavering commitment to method—a disciplined systematical focus of the mind on those things in nature that could be known by observation and experiment and be measured. All knowledge that was not the product of experiment was, for Newton and his Enlightenment colleagues, "feigned"—that is, somehow counterfeit.

Newton is perhaps best known for his law of universal gravitation. The story that he started investigating gravity when an apple hit him in the head while he slept under a tree is probably made up. Throughout human history people took for granted that things fell to the ground if they were left free to fall. Newton's twist on what seemed obvious to everyone was to ask the question, "why do things fall to the earth?" This "why" question opened up a whole new way of thinking about the world, which provided the basis for all of classical mechanics, that is, the study of how all living and nonliving things behave when they move and when they are at rest. Newton's classical mechanics became the foundation for all branches of physics, with practical applications in astronomy, chemistry, and engineering.

Gravity, as Newton discovered, is a force pulling on objects and is everywhere present. Moreover, every object attracts every other object, whether it is a person or any other thing around him or her. The pull of gravity depends on an object's mass—how much matter it has, its density. The greater the mass or matter, the greater its attracting force.

Newton's law of universal gravitation would have been enough to earn him a place as one of the greatest minds in human history. But, in addition to this achievement, he conducted experiments with optics, combining different lenses, prisms, and reflectors, until he was able to design a great telescope with which to observe the stars.

Newton's experiments with optics benefited not only astronomers but also artists because it led to a new understanding of light and color. These experiments involved setting up a prism near a window, such that when the prism caught the sunlight it projected a spectrum of colors onto an opposing wall—violet, indigo, blue, green, yellow, orange, and red. To make sure the prism itself was not adding color to the sunlight, he refracted the light back together into white light. Newton's experiments with color and light fascinated painters. The color wheel he developed was immediately useful to them. Newton arranged the colors around the circumference of a circle such that the primary colors of red, yellow, and blue were opposite their complementary colors—for example, red opposite green—as a way of indicating that each complementarity would intensify the other's effect by way of optical contrast. (See illustration 2.1, Isaac Newton's Color Wheel, at https://www.avemariapress.com/church-and-the-age-of-enlightenment-art.)

Newton was unique among the Enlightenment elite in that he held on to a belief in God, even if it was by the thinnest of cords. In a letter to a clergyman of the Church of England, Newton attributed the precise positioning of the sun and the planets of the solar system to the hand of a grand designer. For example, in explaining why the sun alone among all the satellites in the solar system gave light, he wrote, "Why there is one Body in our System qualified to give Light and Heat to all the rest, I know no Reason, but because the Author of the System thought it convenient."[14]

Proof of a deity, for Newton, also lay in the exact tilt of the Earth's axis, such that even its slight deviation would not support life.

Newton conceded the existence of a designer deity based on such reasoning, but he dismissed a belief in a personal God, specifically the God of revelation, one who intervenes in human affairs and the lives of individuals. Newton conceived of the universe as an immense machine, created by a now absent deity that functions continuously according to its own internally consistent laws without the need of any divine interference.

Newton's achievements dazzled his contemporaries. Seeking to imitate his accomplishments, his disciples seized upon his way of working as the key to their own success. They applied it not only to the physical world, which was the sole focus of Newton's experiments, but also to the human worlds of politics, economics, and religion. Two aspects of Newton's method were particularly important for shaping how the Enlightenment project developed during the late 1600s and 1700s: (1) the redefinition of real knowledge as empirical, mathematical knowledge, which meant that the trustworthiness of knowledge is that which could be known solely by observation, experiment, and measurement; and (2) the recasting of God's relationship to the world as a distant deity.

Inspired by Newton's rigorous empiricism, the Enlightenment generation exhibited a resolute, unprecedented confidence in the possibility of mastering the natural world in the name of progress. It was a noble goal: to make life a little better for everyone. But its champions oversold the idea of continual progress, making immodest claims about the inevitability of human improvement, morally, and materially, and little or no provision for its unintended consequences.

The major figures of the Enlightenment differed on the extent to which Newtonian methods could apply fruitfully to social life, politics, economic, and most of all, religion. Their differences divided the Enlightenment into two camps: the Moderates and the Radicals.

The Moderate Enlightenment

The Moderate Enlightenment was by far more influential than the Radical. Chief among its proponents were David Hume (1711–1776), John Locke (1632–1704), Isaac Newton (1643–1727), and Adam Smith (1723–1790) in Great Britain; René Descartes (1596–1650) in France and the Netherlands; Baron de Montesquieu (1689–1755) and Voltaire, in France; and Kant, Gottfried Wilhelm Leibniz (1646–1716), and Christian Wolff (1679–1745) in the German states. They held comparatively modest views on what reason could actually achieve, and they left space for religious faith in one's personal life, but not in the realm of government and public policy. They often failed to acknowledge the ideas and moral practices they inherited from Christianity, preferring to see them as available to any reasonable mind, unaided by revealed religion. Among these were a divinely ordered cosmos, the divine origin of morality, and the immortality of the soul. Two figures in particular epitomized the Moderate Enlightenment's wide range of interests and influence, Immanuel Kant and Adam Smith.

Immanuel Kant: The Sacredness of Human Autonomy

Kant was a towering intellect. Oddly, although his influence is nearly unrivaled in human history, he rarely traveled much beyond the city of his birth, the Prussian city of Königsberg (which is today Kaliningrad, Russia). He was a man of strict habits and austere self-discipline. According to a famous anecdote, his neighbors set their clock by his daily walk to and from his classes at the University of Königsberg.

Königsberg was a hub of German culture and leading-edge ideas in the eighteenth century, especially in the development and dissemination of Newton's mathematics and physics. A strong influence on Kant and a key figure in advancing Newtonian ideas in Prussia and all of Central Europe was Leonhard Euler (1707–1783). Euler's contributions to mathematics was second only to Newton's. Among his more popular achievements was the standardization of mathematical notation that is still in use today. But it was the physical geography of Königsberg that occasioned one of Euler's groundbreaking mathematical achievements.

Euler took on the challenge of a long-standing mathematical puzzle with the folksy label of "The Problem of Königsberg Seven Bridges." (See illustration 2.2, "The Problem of the Seven Bridges" at https://www.ave mariapress.com/church-and-the-age-of-enlightenment-art.) Seven bridges spanned the Pregel river, connecting Königsberg to the surrounding countryside. The challenge to anyone willing to take it on was to map out a walk through the city that would cross each of the seven bridges only once. The puzzle had no solution. To prove it Euler developed two new branches of mathematics, graph theory and topology. Graphs are mathematical models that represent relations between objects. Topology, not to be confused with topography, is the study of the properties of objects when they are at rest, which allowed Euler to apply Newton's calculus in a new and innovative way.

Euler was among the men who set the agenda for Kant's lifelong project, which was to explore the implications of Newton's mechanical worldview for philosophy. Kant used Newton to mathematize human reasoning, which meant building a new foundation for knowledge that would make it dependable and certain, and devoid of speculation. The result was his celebrated trilogy that changed the course of philosophical inquiry: *The Critique of Pure Reason* (1787), *The Critique of Practical Reason* (1788), and *The Critique of Judgment* (1790). Each of these books systematically cleared away the received thinking about truth, goodness, and beauty— the ultimate, unchanging desires of the heart—and erected new standards for understanding them.

Christian thinking and classical philosophy referred to truth, goodness, and beauty as transcendentals—properties of the spiritual or nonphysical world of human existence. Christianity, especially, has always taught that all three are found in God and attained by both faith and reason. Kant closed off the road of faith and insisted that reason alone was sufficient to attain them, but in a much more limited way than Christianity had taught. Indeed, for Kant, resorting to faith to fully understand truth, goodness, and beauty was morally irresponsible, an example of pre-Enlightenment immaturity. For Kant, falling back on faith, or the Christian belief in the interdependence of faith and reason, violated human dignity. Faith required some measure of trusting something or someone beyond one's own powers of rigorous reasoning. Human dignity, for Kant, rested on the moral imperative of thinking for oneself.

"Dare to think," was the motto Kant applied to the Enlightenment program. Independent thinking summed up the Enlightenment intellectual program and underlined its very essence, the full autonomy and independence of each person. Everything he or she had learned from family, teachers, and country had to be subjected to the most rigorous critical analysis before accepting them as true. The role of government was to create the conditions whereby such free thinking flourished with little or no interference.

Because human reasoning, like mathematical formulas, is universal, Kant had great faith that right-thinking individuals would come to some sort of consensus about the common good of society. In short, while "dare to think" celebrated human freedom of a sort, its emphasis on human autonomy masked a form of skepticism, which cast suspicion on faith, tradition, received wisdom, and in general other minds, whether past or present.

Thinking for oneself was especially important in matters of religion. Kant's commitment to German pietism, which emphasized the individual experience of religious feeling, corresponded with the autonomy he celebrated in the use of reason. As a devout Pietist, Kant was averse to ecclesiastical and governmental constraints on religious thought, mainly because it provoked civil strife. The Thirty Years' War was within living memory of Kant's generation, and it lingered as a persistent and traumatic reminder of this tendency. Although Königsberg did not experience the degree of destruction that other areas of Germany did, the war forced two prominent Calvinist dynastic families, the Houses of Hohenzollern and Wittelsbach, to take refuge in Königsberg. Kant lived in the aftermath of the tension between the Lutherans of Königsberg and the refuge Calvinist royalty and their followers.

But beyond the civil unrest caused by religious differences, Kant believed that restricting or in any way constraining how one chose to think about religion was a grave violation of human dignity because it infringed on the sacredness of a person's intellect and will in the most essential aspect of what it means to be human: religious belief and commitment.

Kant insisted that government had no business meddling in the salvation of its people. The role of government was "to prevent one man from forcibly keeping another from determining and promoting his salvation to the best of his ability."[15] But more to the point, a government degraded itself when it supported "the sort of despotism of a few tyrants in [its] sovereign power over the rest of its citizens."[16] The lesson that Kant drew from the Thirty Years' War was that above any other sphere of human activity and belief, governments will always want to interfere with the religious beliefs of their citizens because they are the core of their humanity. If governments control religion, they control everything.

Adam Smith: The Law of the Hidden Hand

Adam Smith was an exact contemporary of Kant and a prominent member of the Scottish Enlightenment. Like Kant, the thinkers of the Scottish Enlightenment celebrated human reason and rejected any authority or tradition that could not justify itself solely by the standards of rigorous reasoning. Like Newton and Kant, Smith's commitment to advancing the Enlightenment program was so complete that he never married.

Smith's upbringing was thoroughly middle class. His family lived in a small town about twelve miles north of Edinburgh, Scotland. In an otherwise uneventful boyhood, an early biographer reported that when Smith was four years old, gypsies abducted him. He was rescued by a passerby who noticed a gypsy woman holding the inconsolable baby Smith. The passerby signaled for help, at which point the woman dropped the child and the boy was returned to his mother. The biographer noted wryly, "[Smith] would have made, I fear, a poor gypsy."

Smith spent most of his career as a professor of moral philosophy at the University of Glasgow. Before he earned a permanent academic appointment, he wrote and lectured under the auspices of the Philosophical Society of Edinburgh, one of the many societies, clubs, and organizations founded during the Enlightenment to advance the Enlightenment agenda. These societies were crucially important for disseminating the ideas and the culture of the Enlightenment and associating them with the chic world of European salon and café society.

Smith's most famous work, *An Inquiry into the Nature and Causes of the Wealth of Nations* (1776), generally shortened to *The Wealth of Nations*, earned him the titles of Father of Economics and Father of Capitalism. Smith's book challenged prevailing notions of how nations measured their financial health. In describing how wealth was created, he shifted the focus from the actions of governments to the actions of individuals. Smith invented the well-known idea of the invisible or hidden hand, by which individuals working independently to advance their self-interest actually and unintentionally advanced the interests of society and raised the standard of living for all. The mysterious behavior of the free market de facto became the measure of the common good. No one planned it, no one directed it. It just would happen.

The doctrine of the hidden hand, for Smith, was more a moral concept than an economic one. It is nowhere present in *The Wealth of Nations* but is prominently featured in his less famous book *The Theory of Moral Sentiments* (1759). The notion of "goods" was literal for Smith. The things produced in a society were in fact good things for people to have in order to thrive and necessary to raise the standard of living for all citizens, not just society's upper crust. Producing and distributing goods and services efficiently and widely required the discovery and expression of the universal laws of human behavior. Such was Smith's project.

The sphere of economics for Smith included how people work, how they earn their money, how they buy and sell, and how the government supervises all this activity. It was in his idealized view a world of peaceful competition for the benefit of everyone. Like Newton's Laws of Nature, the economy in Smith's formulation obeyed certain universal laws applicable everywhere and at all times.

Fundamental to these laws was Smith's reconception of what made humans unique in the order of creation. In his reckoning, human beings are essentially traders. At the root of economic activity, is the human tendency "to truck, barter, and exchange one thing for another."[17] Human reason and language enabled this tendency, which is present nowhere else in creation. Smith wrote, "Nobody ever saw a dog make a fair and deliberate exchange of one bone for another with another dog. Nobody ever saw one animal by its gestures and natural cries signify to another, that is mine, that yours; I am willing to give this for that."[18]

From this observation about the human urge to trade, Smith built the entire system of free market economics. Its purposes were "to provide a plentiful revenue or subsistence for the people, or more properly to provide such a revenue or subsistence for themselves; and secondly to supply the state or commonwealth with a revenue sufficient for the public services. It [the free market] proposes to enrich both the people and the sovereign."[19]

The Radical Enlightenment

The main secular competitor to the Moderate Enlightenment was the Radical Enlightenment. It occupied the fringes of the Enlightenment project. Its prominent figures were Baruch Spinoza (1632–1677) in the

Netherlands; Pierre Bayle (1647–1784), Denis Diderot (1713–1784), and Nicolas de Condorcet (1743–1794) in France; and Thomas Paine (1737–1809) in America. They were skeptical about the power of faith or reason to understand the world. What united them was the conviction that tradition, history, the past, and received authority were obstacles to establishing a new society. They were materialist, egalitarian, and anti-religious, and vigorously bucked any resistance to their anti-traditionalist agenda. They were largely a quasi-clandestine group, not really an organized force. Nonetheless, they persistently disrupted the Moderate program. In the nineteenth and twentieth centuries, Marxists claimed the Radical Enlightenment as the origin of their movement. What follows is a brief profile of two of the more influential Radical Enlighteners, who typified Radical Enlightenment thinking: Pierre Bayle and Thomas Paine.

Pierre Bayle: The Master of Doubt

Pierre Bayle's parents were French Calvinists, long settled in the Ariège region in southwest France near the foothills of the Pyrenees Mountains. The region was renowned for its lush, scenic landscape. Bayle's father educated him at home, with supplemental instruction provided by a nearby boys academy. Bayle converted to Catholicism at age twenty-two while studying at a Jesuit university in Toulouse a generation before Fr. Caussade taught there. But shortly afterward he reverted to Calvinism and left France for Geneva, Switzerland, the center of Calvinist thought in Europe.

Bayle's reversion to Calvinism came with a new conviction that there was little humans could know by faith or reason. He rejected the notion that humans could know anything with certainty. Thus, any doctrine, whether religious or secular, was untruthful because nothing could be known or believed with certainty. Furthermore, to compel anyone to believe what was in reality an illusion of truth was an act of tyranny and injustice. For Bayle, the only way to live amid such thought was to cultivate the virtues of toleration and forbearance—the prominent themes of his writings.

Among the philosophes, moderate and radical, only Newton received greater admiration than Bayle. One of his radical contemporaries praised him for teaching a new generation how to doubt. The moderates worried about Bayle's extreme skepticism about the power of reason, but they savored his savage critique of what he saw as superstition and religious fanaticism.

All of Bayle's writings were required reading for all philosophes, chiefly his *Diverse Thoughts on Halley's Comet* (1682), which was Bayle's first book and a classic example of Radical Enlightenment thinking. The reappearance of Halley's Comet in autumn 1680 was a welcome opportunity for Newton to test his new law of universal gravitation. But for many others it was an omen of the approaching end times. People thronged to their churches to pray for deliverance, and government and religious leaders declared days of fasting to forestall the terror of a reckoning.

On the surface, Bayle's book was a condemnation of fanatical superstition and an obvious attack on the Catholic Church. Read this way, Bayle's *Diverse Thoughts* was one more contribution to the conflict between Catholics and Protestants, and rational philosophes and religious believers. But a deeper reading of the book reveals something else, the Enlightenment's most explicit rejection of inherited knowledge and the value of history as a mean to the discovery of truth. Here's why.

In the book, Bayle reviewed in detail the long history of comets and their association with ominous events to come. His history began with the first account of comets among the ancient Greeks and Romans and continued with every siting up to his own time. Bayle's real purpose in providing these historical accounts was to dethrone the power of authority. In this case not the authority of living statesmen and churchmen but the authority of writers up and down the centuries. To Bayle, it was obvious that pre-Enlightenment theologians, philosophers, historians, and other writers, whether knowing or not, encouraged and sustained humanity's anxiety about the appearance of comets. Men and women took it on faith what other people before them had written without critically examining their writings.

Bayle's main argument is that writings of previous ages were merely the physical remains of different eras, thinking, and circumstances, all of which held no meaning for modern times and could even be dangerous. Pre-Enlightenment beliefs about comets were as unsound as beliefs in numerology and astrology. For Bayle, the seventeenth century was entirely different from what had gone before, all of which he considered an unenlightened primitive past. To believe in what seemed to be factual evidence written by premodern writers was wrongheaded and would continue to contribute to an uncritical acceptance of superstitious beliefs and practices and hamper the progress of humanity that was at the core of the Enlightenment program.

At the end of the day, Bayle's book is more than an attack on religion. It is radical skepticism at its height, an assault on the truth of history. Bayle delegitimized the past and thereby provided a key argument for reconstituting the whole world as if it were a blank slate, whereby nothing that came before was trustworthy enough to depend on.

Thomas Paine: The Utopianism of the Radical Enlightenment

Thomas Paine was an Englishman but found his true calling as the most radical voice of the American Revolution of 1776. Since the 1500s, Europeans idealized America as a land for starting over, a veritable blank slate. John Locke, in his famous *Second Treatise of Government* (1699), wrote, "In the beginning, all the world was America." America was an opportunity for new beginnings unburdened by the drag of the past. Of course, America was not really a blank slate; its indigenous peoples had lived there for millennia and built great civilizations. Like all human societies they had remarkable achievements and vicious practices. Nevertheless, the stories and depictions of American natives that circulated among sixteenth- and seventeenth-century Europeans inspired idyllic representations of what life was like in an uncorrupted state of nature. Indeed, Paine's report on his meeting with the Iroquois affirmed this idyll. He marveled at their seemingly harmonious way of living in accord with nature and their democratic system for making major decisions.

Before his emigration to America, Paine spent his boyhood in a small village in Norfolk County on the east coast of England. His father was a Quaker; his mother, Anglican. Paine attended the village grammar school when such schooling was not compulsory. At thirteen he took up his father's trade as a corset maker. When the family's corset shop failed and Paine's first wife and their child died during childbirth, he left Norfolk and lived a nomadic life earning a living successively as a shopkeeper, a civil servant, and a teacher.

His career as an activist began in 1772, when he led a group of customs officers (then called excise officers) in their demands for better pay and working conditions. He published a twelve-page pamphlet titled *The Case of the Officers of Excise*, for which he was dismissed from service in 1774. Following his dismissal, a commissioner of the Excise Service, George Lewis Scott, befriended Paine. Scott's government work supplied him a salary that financed his real interest in mathematics, a field in which he excelled to the point of becoming a Fellow of the prestigious Royal Society. Scott introduced Paine into the society, where he met Benjamin Franklin. Paine and Franklin hit it off immediately, so much so that Franklin paid for Paine to move to Philadelphia in 1774, where Paine become a prominent leader in the colonial revolt against Great Britain.

Although historians are rightly wary of asking "what if" questions about the past, such alternative histories often prompt imaginative and illuminating fiction. In the case of Paine, absent his arrival in America and his stridently Radical Enlightenment philosophy, the American colonials might well have reached an accord with Great Britain that would have prevented armed revolt. Less than a year after he stepped onto the Philadelphia docks, Paine published *Common Sense* (1775), advocating American independence from Great Britain. Written in a popular style with none of the dense, technical philosophical language of many other philosophes, *Common Sense* urged everyday Americans to resist and overthrow the rule of King George III, when only a minority of them entertained seriously the idea of independence from Great Britain.

Common Sense was an immediate success. Ordinary folks purchased it and read it aloud in taverns and meeting halls up and down the Eastern Seaboard of North America. Based on the population of the thirteen colonies in 1776 (about 2.5 million people), *Common Sense* still holds the record for the largest sales and circulation of any book published in the United States. It was the most provocative and incendiary written work of the entire Revolutionary period, and an example of the Radical Enlightenment in action. Paine's brilliance was to connect the clean-slate thinking of the Enlightenment with the tradition of Protestant dissent and the utopianism of its extremist offshoots. Paine argued that the existence of government was a constant reminder of lost innocence. "We have it in our power," wrote Paine, "to begin the world over again. A situation similar to the present has not happened since the days of Noah until now."[20]

Paine's biblical references here and elsewhere resonated in unison with devote New England Puritans, who delighted in comparing their flight from Britain to Israel's exodus from Egypt. Like the Israelites, the Puritans celebrated their errand into the wilderness to establish a new land in the early 1600s. After the success of the American revolt against England, his Puritan admirers were horrified to learn that Paine despised all established religion. In the *Age of Reason*, published in the mid-1790s during the heady excitement of the French Revolution, Paine wrote:

> I do not believe in the creed professed by the Jewish church, by the Roman church, by the Greek church, by the Turkish church, by the Protestant church, nor by any church that I know of.

> My own mind is my own church. All churches, whether Jew-
> ish, Christian or Turkish, appear to me no other than human
> inventions, set up to terrify and enslave mankind, and monop-
> olize power and profit.[21]

Paine's blueprint for a new, utopian society included idealized notions of self-government, a strong faith in the inevitability of scientific and social progress, a commitment to Adam Smith's model of free markets, and Kant's autonomous individualism. He took what were essentially Moderate Enlightenment ideas and extended their logic to form a vision of a future redeemed by political messianism, whose first fruits were the American and French Revolutions. For Paine, the new Enlightenment person would be the Adam of a new world, without need of religion.

Up Close and Personal:

ST. MARIE OF THE INCARNATION (1599–1672)

The life of St. Marie of the Incarnation illustrates dramatically how the contemplative practice of abandonment to Divine Providence led to an energetic active life of missionary zeal. Her life harmonized the contemplative vocation typically associated with the cloister and astonishing practical accomplishments. Among her many achievements was the founding of the Ursuline monastery of Quebec in 1639, the oldest institution of learning for women in North America. She modeled her life on St. Teresa of Avila. She identified so closely with St. Teresa's *Autobiography* and imitated her life so thoroughly that the most influential French cleric and preacher of her day, Bishop Jacques-Bénigne Bossuet (1627–1704), called her the St. Teresa of her time and of the Americas.

Marie was the fourth of eight children born to Florent and Jeanne Guyart in Tours, France. Her family had deep roots in the French aristocracy, with claims to an ancestry that dated back to the period of St. Martin (316–397). St. Martin, the third bishop of Tours, made the city famous for his great charity, captured in the well-known story of the sharing of his cloak with a naked beggar. Marie was a pious girl. At fourteen she asked her parents for permission to enter a nearby Benedictine cloister. But they thought the contemplative life ill-suited to her outgoing personality and lively interest in French culture. Instead, they married Marie to a silk worker who died while their son was still an infant. She took up domestic work to support her son and her aging father. In 1620, when she was in her early twenties, she encountered the writings of St. Teresa of Avila and had a profound conversion to the religious life.

She joined the Ursulines, entrusting her son to the Jesuits. He would eventually join the Benedictines and become his mother's first biographer. In 1639, Marie departed France with a small group of sisters to establish a convent and school in Quebec. Her missionary work became closely connected with the history of France in the Americas. She was a formidable businesswoman and adept in legal matters. She drew up contracts and defended her rights against French settlers who tried to take her crown-granted privileges away from her.

St. Marie had clear ideas about how the economy of New France should develop. She took a keen interest in the discovery of mineral resources. In establishing her convent and school, Marie operated a farm, dug wells, and ran a bakery. Colonial governors and other leaders often sought out her counsel. She was also a skilled diplomat, mediating relations between the French colonists and the Iroquois, Huron, and Algonquin tribes.

Alongside all of this activity she sustained a deep interior life of prayer, which she described in letters to her son, Dom Claude Martin. Dom Claude edited and published these letters along with Marie's pre-missionary spiritual diaries of the 1620s.

He organized these diaries to correspond with the stages of contemplative progress outlined by St. Teresa of Avila: purification, illumination, and union with God. They were published in the 1650s as *Retreats of Venerable Mother Marie of the Incarnation*. This work, along with the unpublished, privately circulated retreat conferences of Fr. Caussade and other such writings, became a spiritual counterculture to the increasing secularism of the Enlightenment.

The Convergence of the Moderates and Radicals

By the twentieth century, the major differences between the Moderate and Radical Enlightenment faded. What they shared in common was ultimately far greater than the little that made them different in the seventeenth century. Although some among the moderate camp continued to profess a belief in God, their philosophy emptied the idea of God of its traditional content. In realty, both strains of the Enlightenment pretty much abandoned religion as a source of meaning. The Enlightenment undermined the validity of Europe's spiritual vision. As a result, it narrowed the breadth of what it meant to be truly human to the strictly rational. Mind became the hardware that ran the software of calculating rationalism and established life's meaning and values.

The visual arts, literature, and music of the Enlightenment era reflect this new view of the human person. Rarely did the artists, poets, and composers of the Enlightenment period rival the explosive creativity of the Renaissance of the fifteenth century. The great musical achievement of composers of the seventeenth and eighteenth centuries, such as George Frideric Handel (1685–1759), Johann Sebastian Bach (1685–1750), and

Franz Joseph Haydn (1732–1809), more often than not drew on the Christian resources of the pre-Enlightenment for their compositions.

A World Devoid of Mystery and Sacredness

A common criticism of the Enlightenment is that it sapped the world of its mystery. The outlook of two near contemporizes of the age of Enlightenment, Sir Isaac Newton and Fr. Jean-Pierre de Caussade, illustrate this critique. Just before his death Newton said, "I don't know what I may seem to the world, but, as to myself, I seem to have been only like a boy playing on the sea-shore, and diverting myself in now and then finding a smoother pebble or a prettier shell than ordinary, whilst the great ocean of truth lay all undiscovered before me."[22] There is certain delight in the playfulness with which Newton thought of his life's work and an exhilaration in the thrill of discovery. But ultimately, for Newton, the thrill was the mind coming to understand and master the vast undiscovered universe. It was the journey of the world into the mind of man.

While there is much that is good and noble in Newton's project, it breaks sharply from how men and women before him stood before the great mysteries of the world. In the midst of the Enlightenment, Caussade reenergized the action of faith as the interpreter of the boundless mystery of the universe. Aware of the Enlightenment's enshrinement of reason, he encouraged a stance before the universe and each moment of life that acknowledged the limits of reason, beyond which is the mysterious voice of God. Caussade equated understanding the presence of God in the present moment with reading the Word of God. The present moment for him complemented scripture. He wrote:

> How ought we to listen to the word which is spoken to us in
> the depth of our hearts at every moment? If our sense and our
> reason do not understand or penetrate the truth and goodness
> of that word, is it not on account of their incapacity for divine

truths? Should I be astonished because a mystery disconcerts my reason? God Speaks: it is a mystery. . . . A mystery is life to the heart through faith, but for the rest of our faculties a contradiction.[23]

In a delicious and perhaps unintended play on the Enlightenment's self-satisfaction with its own lights, Caussade offered a paradox, a puzzle: "The darker the mystery, the more light it contains."[24] To be sure there are echoes of Carmelite contemplative practice in these words—St. John of the Cross's *Dark Night of the Soul*, for example. But there is also the influence of St. Francis de Sales, who reached sanctity as bishop of Geneva a battleground between Calvinists and Catholics in the immediate aftermath of the Protestant revolt. It was the city in which Bayle developed his profound skepticism of the truths of reason and faith.

A Doctor of the Church, St. Francis was an extremely well-educated man from a noble family headed for a career in civil law, but he decided instead to follow a call to the priesthood. His theology developed against the immediate and intense pressures of Calvinism and the nascent scientific revolution that preceded and helped spur the Enlightenment. As a man fully aware and accomplished in the possibilities and potential of human reason, St. Francis advanced the certainty of faith, which in a short hymn to faith he characterized as a "black beauty."

> O faith, you are the great friend of our spirit, and to the human sciences which boast that they are more evident than you can well sat what the Spouse said to her companions: "I am black but beautiful." You are black because you are in the obscurity of the divine revelations, which have no apparent evidence, make you appear *black*, and most unrecognizable; but yet you are *beautiful* in yourself because of your infinite certainty.[25]

This chapter focused mainly on ideas, which were what the Enlightenment was all about. Its leading figures were passionate about ideas—but less so about the rest of what made life worth living: authentic religiosity (not its caricature), art, music, literature, and poetry. The Enlightenment was one of the great movements of societal renewal among many such movements in Europe and America. It differed from previous movements in its contempt for history and its near-total disregard for what a thoroughgoing secularity meant for the culture of the West. The next chapter reveals what the Enlightenment ignored: the cultural achievements inspired by Christianity, which have always accompanied great periods of renewal in Western civilization.

YOU BE THE JUDGE:

Was the Enlightenment project heretical?

Earlier in this chapter we read Christopher Dawson's assertion that the Enlightenment was the last of the great European heresies. What is the substance of such a claim?

For people serious about their religious beliefs, heresy can be a serious charge. The origin of the English word *heresy* means simply a choice one makes and a commitment to that choice. In the Catholic tradition, a choice becomes heretical when a baptized person obstinately rejects a dogma or other truth defined by the Catholic Church. In this strict sense of heresy, Dawson's claim seems to be an exaggeration. But the Church has always recognized degrees of heresy. The Enlightenment project taken in its totality was never formally declared heretical by the Catholic Church. Nevertheless, there are certain elements of Enlightenment thinking that if taken to their logical ends would be variance with revealed truth. The Church would consider such lines of thought *hæresi proxima* (next to heresy). For example, the Church teaches that there can be no conflict between faith and reason, that reason properly used and faith properly understood will never produce contradictory claims. John Locke, a leading Enlightenment thinker, in an effort to make the Christian faith reasonable, stressed the reasonableness of faith to such a degree that if a religious doctrine conflicted with known facts, it signaled its unsoundness. This line of reasoning would thereby reject doctrines such as the Trinity and the Real Presence of Jesus because they could not be justified by reason.

The Enlightenment disjoining of faith and reason has consequences for such fundamental Christian virtues as charity and human flourishing. Pope Benedict XVI in his 2009 encyclical *Caritas in Veritate* points out that "truth is the light that gives meaning and value to charity. That light is both the light of reason and the light of faith, through which the intellect attains to the natural and supernatural truth of charity: it grasps its meaning as gift, acceptance, and communion" (3). Pope Benedict does not merely affirm the complementarity of faith and reason but underscores the purifying effect each one has on the other and the harmful consequences for humanity when they are cut off from each other.

> *Reason always stands in need of being purified by faith*: this also holds true for political reason, which must not consider itself omnipotent. For its part, *religion always needs to be purified by reason* in order to show its authentically human face. Any breach in this dialogue comes only at an enormous price to human development. . . . Faced with these dramatic questions, reason and faith can come to each other's assistance. Only together will they save man. *Entranced by an exclusive reliance on technology, reason without faith is doomed to flounder in an illusion of its own omnipotence. Faith without reason risks being cut off from everyday life.* (*Caritas in Veritate* 56, 74; Pope Benedict's italics)

It is important to remember that the "technology" referenced by Pope Benedict was the practical result of the Enlightenment's enthusiasm for a mathematized mode of reasoning. To be sure, such use of reason has produced benefits to humankind. But consider Pope Benedict's warning about "the illusion of omnipotence" associated with the Enlightenment's severing of reason from faith as a way of knowing. Could Dawson be right? Was the Enlightenment in some sense heretical?

Chapter 3

The Religious Enlightenment

The Night of Fire: A Portrait of Blaise Pascal

How does a person come to faith, and what does that faith know? These are questions for the ages. But under pressure from the Enlightenment's cult of reason, they became especially vivid for Christians. The life and work of Blaise Pascal (1623–1662) offers unique and enduring insights into these questions. For in him coexisted the heady buzz of the Enlightenment's scientific self-consciousness and an earnest and passionate Christian faith.

Pascal was a pioneering mathematician of the highest rank, a physicist, an astronomer, and a brilliant defender of the experimental sciences. He was a child prodigy, the Wolfgang Amadeus Mozart of mathematics, who as a boy traveled in the elite circles of European mathematicians. Pascal's original contributions to geometry were so impressive that word of them reached the great René Descartes, the founder of analytic geometry, who briefly marveled at them and then dismissed them as still boyish.

Pascal's father, Etienne, a widower and tax collector in Rouen, early on had recognized his son's talent and educated him at home. Always a sensitive soul, Blaise eased his father's mentally numbing work of endless paper and pen calculations of tax bills and receipts by inventing the first calculating machine. Blaise built fifty of these calculators, which never found a commercial market. The guild of quill-driving government clerks resisted its use—so much for technological progress. Nevertheless, many computer scientists and engineers of the twenty-first century regard them as forerunners of their fields.

While the Pascals did not suffer any direct physical violence of the Thirty Years' War, it indirectly caused their financial ruin. In order to finance France's two-front war against the Austrian and Spanish Habsburgs during the fourth phase of the Thirty Years' War, Cardinal Richelieu deliberately defaulted on the government bonds that made up the majority of Etienne's financial holdings. Etienne protested and became an outspoken opponent of Richelieu's fiscal policies, after which he had to flee Paris, leaving Blaise and his two younger sisters with a neighbor, the infamous Madame Sainctot.

Madame Sainctot was an elegant and charming woman of great influence, who hosted one of the most fashionable cultural and intellectual salons in France. Her flirtatiousness once made her the target of an assassination plot hatched by a rival for the affections of a prominent French duke. The assassin was the infamous professional poisoner, Marguerite Joly (1637–1681), who also just happened to be Madame Sainctot's sister-in-law.

Madame Sainctot introduced Blaise to salon life, which was very much to his liking. Its high intrigue and constant merriment were for a time his joie de vivre and his introduction to games of chance, to which he developed something just short of an obsession. Its happy by-product was his invention of modern probability theory and the formulation of his famous wager on the Christian life. Pascal argued that a reasonable person ought to behave as if God exists and cultivate a belief in him. If God does not actually exist, this person's losses would be finite, such as pleasure, luxury, and power. But if God does indeed exist, such a person stands to gain infinite benefits, eternal life with God and a resurrected body, and he or she had avoided an infinite loss, eternal damnation. Although to some Pascal's wager might seem a crass defense of Christianity, Pascal was in part following his theological hero, St. Augustine of Hippo, who taught that acting as if one believes, after a while, generates authentic faith.

During Pascal's early thirties, at the height of his success and notoriety, and while enjoying the high life of French society, he underwent a profound spiritual malaise. He had something like the experience Newton had just before his death, a relentlessly inquisitive mind standing in fear and trembling before a vast ocean of undiscovered truth. Pascal put it this way: "The eternal silence of this infinite space frightens me."[1] How had the cosmos come into existence? Why this great void? How puzzling was the crown of creation, the human person!

These questions drove Pascal into a deep depression, which he defeated by a profound reconversion to his cradle Catholicism. Had not his servant discovered a parchment sewn into Pascal's coat following Pascal's death, we may never have known how dramatically he came to faith and vanquished his interior darkness. The parchment was enfolded around a faded piece of paper with the unassuming title of "Mémorial." With great precision "Mémorial" recorded the time and date of when Pascal emerged from his dark night with a certainty about faith as a means of knowing and a participation in the mind of God. It was "the night of fire," Monday, November 23, 1654, between 10:30 p.m. and just past midnight. Pascal also noted the liturgical time: "The feast of Saint Clement, pope and martyr and others in the martyrology. The eve of Saint Chrysogonous martyr and others." Then followed sequences of heartfelt eruptions of praise and impassioned insights.

> Fire
> The God of Abraham, the God of Isaac, the God of Jacob
> Not of the philosophers and intellectuals
> Certitude, certitude, feeling, joy, peace
> The God of Jesus[2]

"Mémorial" continued with this tone of joy and certainty for no more than a page. The night of fire was a deeply private, life-changing event for Pascal. He handwrote several copies of "Mémorial," sewing them into the lining of each new coat he wore. He did not share this momentous event with anyone. His life continued seamlessly, integrating the mind of the scientist with a hard-won, grace-filled conviction of the truth of Catholicism.

Emphatically, Pascal's epiphanic assent of mind, body, and soul to the Christian faith was not therapeutic. It was not a sudden cure for his depression. Rather, it was foremost a confession of the limits of reason, and the recognition that faith is the only way of knowing the mystery beyond what human knowledge can grasp—"the eternal silence" of the infinite space that frightened Pascal. Moreover, Pascal's certitude of faith was not abstract and general, but particular. It was faith in the God of Abraham, Isaac, and Jacob. In other words, it was the biblical revelation of God, which is the story of God's action in human history. It is difficult to overstate Pascal's insight here. The Enlightenment philosophes rejected the idea of God's intervention in human history. For them God was present at the beginning to set the universe in motion but is now unavailable to humans.

Sacred scripture contradicted this view. Christianity is nothing if not a historical religion. Pascal's ultimate embrace of Jesus Christ signified his recognition that God intervened in human history in the most dramatic way, by becoming human.

Finally, although Pascal's night of fire brought him great joy and perhaps some consolation. It was not the sort of consolation that secured him against further mental anguish. His dramatic and fervent embrace of the Christian faith in the midst of a rapidly secularizing culture set him on a course in which he would have to confront an intensely disquieting intellectual opposition.

Alongside his world-class achievements in mathematics and the sciences, Pascal also created two enduring, if not widely appreciated, concepts, which corrected two problematic aspects of the Enlightenment. His concept of *finesse* pushed back against scientific overreach, which involved the application of mathematics and the scientific method to all aspects of life, including the human person. The second was *heart*, which opposed the reduction of the human person to mind alone. Pascal distinguished between the geometric mind and the intuitive mind. The former works with precise definition, measurable objects, and evidence; the latter, with ideas and perceptions that evade exact definition and measurement. For example, a right-angle triangle and Newton's universal law of gravitation are perfectly definite concepts. Poetry, love, and sound government do not submit themselves to the same kind of exactness. The lack of mathematical precision in the case of intuition is not because a person does not have correct information; rather, its cause is the very nature of the subject itself. Moreover, the rational, mathematical mind is not immune from imprecision and mistakes. Consensus among scientists is difficult to achieve. Scientists are continuously revising their declarations and often disagree with each other.

The overreach of the Enlightenment project was predictable. The blood lust of the Thirty Years' War launched its search for unanimity of belief and the canceling of religious and political divisions. But, as Pascal pointed out, this overreach led to the fallacy of scientism, which insists that the methods of experimental science can be applied to all forms of experience and that, given enough time, they will settle all issues. Scientism is an ideology driven by a single-minded quest for certainty in all areas of human existence.

Pascal's second enduring concept, his understanding of *heart*, is emphatically not a reaction to the Enlightenment cult of reason. *Heart* does not elevate feeling over thinking. Rather, for Pascal, it is the spiritual center of a person's being, a person made in the image of God, his or her truest and deepest self. *Heart* recalls the ancient Hebrew idea of *heart* as the unity of the human person—intellectual, feeling, will, and intuition. Heart is not an irrational feeling; rather, it values personal experience and a certain logic that flows from the desires of the heart, thus Pascal's widely quoted passage: "The heart has its reasons that the reason does not know." Here Pascal uses reason in two ways. The first is the reasons of the heart, its needs and motive, which are not products of reason as intellect, the second kind of reasoning. Otherwise there would be no immediate empathy with another, no friendship or love in the world. Pascal left behind scattered insights collected posthumously as *Pensees*, which bear witness to his efforts to reconstruct human personhood—head and heart—against the Enlightenment's tendency to sever them.

The Religious Enlightenment

The great Catholic figures profiled thus far—St. Vincent de Paul, Fr. Jean-Pierre de Caussade, St. Mary of the Incarnation, and Blaise Pascal—were not anti-Enlightenment warriors, nor did they seek any accommodation with it. The Enlightenment weighed lightly in the background of their life and work. Taken together, they were a sort of a spiritual underground, but not intentionally so. Their aim was not to undo the Enlightenment or to stridently challenge its principles but rather to continue their apostolic and intellectual work acknowledging that a new worldview was emerging around them. At times they would have to reframe traditional Catholic ideas to reflect the reality of this new worldview. But they never gutted the essential teaching and experience of Catholicism.

Yet there were other religious figures of the Enlightenment whose aim was a deliberate, full-on engagement and, at times, a conscious accommodation with the Enlightenment project. They could be considered a third branch of the Enlightenment alongside the Moderates and Radicals. They were, in fact, a Religious Enlightenment, and it architects were William Warburton (1698–1779), an Anglican churchman and theologian; Jacob Vernet (1698–1789), a Swiss, Calvinist theologian; Siegmund Jakob Baumgarten (1706–1757), a German Lutheran Pietist theologian; Moses Mendelssohn (1729–1786), a German-Jewish philosopher and the most prominent figure of Haskalah, the Jewish Enlightenment; Joseph Valentin Eybel (1741–1805), an Austrian, Catholic canon lawyer and civil servant; and Adrien Lamourette (1742–1794), a French priest of the Society of St. Vincent de Paul. These men were committed reformers of their religious traditions—Anglican, Calvinist, Lutheran, Jewish, and Catholic—and actively engaged Enlightenment ideas in the mainstream of European intellectual life and culture.

The lure of the secular Enlightenment as a source of religious reform for the Religious Enlighteners was understandable. The scandal of Christians killing each other during the Thirty Years' War brought about widespread religious apostasy among ordinary Catholic and Protestant Europeans. "A plague on both your houses" was not an uncommon sentiment among those who suffered firsthand the plundering of Catholic and Protestant soldiers. During and after the war, education, and particularly religious education in Europe, had almost disappeared, especially in the German states. Seventeenth-century Europeans had become crude in their manners, disrespectful of life and law, and superstitious, as witnessed by frequent burning of witches.

Against this dismal backdrop, two figures of the Religious Enlightenment are particularly compelling: Moses Mendelssohn and Joseph Eybel. Mendelssohn is significant because he led a new movement of Jewish engagement with the wider European culture, made possible by the Peace of Westphalia. He also reclaimed the Bible's spiritual and cultural authority for people of all faiths. Eybel's significance proceeds from his use of Enlightenment ideas about the sovereignty of nation-states to undermine

Catholic Austria's traditional allegiance to the pope and what remained of Europe's spiritual unity.

Moses Mendelssohn and the Haskalah

The eighteenth-century Haskalah (or Jewish Enlightenment) originated in the desire among European Jews to reclaim the Bible, Jewish philosophy, and the Hebrew language. The Haskalah was a European-wide movement, extending from the Baltic regions of northern European to London. It energetically engaged with Enlightenment science and philosophy to create an understanding of Judaism more comprehensible to non-Jews and to improve the social and political position of Jews in early modern Europe. Moses Mendelssohn was the premiere representative of the Haskalah ("from Moses unto Moses there was none like Moses")[3] and a major figure of the Berlin Enlightenment. His voluminous and well-respected writings in the sciences, literature, art, biblical scholarship, and philosophy earned him the title "Socrates of Berlin."

As a religious minority out of the mainstream of European religious life, the Haskalah worked at a disadvantage. For one thing, in post-Westphalia Europe Catholics and Protestants each had strong government support for the institutions that supported and advanced education and culture. The Jews lacked governmental patronage of their universities and academies, and the media and institutions that made up the public sphere, such as journals, newspapers, coffeehouses, and voluntary associations. Instead, the Haskalah had to depend on the irregular sponsorship of successful Jewish merchants and Jews who had made it into the courts of Christian rulers.

The inspiration for those who established the Haskalah was their own ignorance of the biblical foundations of European culture. They thought of themselves as "orphans of knowledge" and set for themselves a first task of assembling a Haskalah library of science, literature, and philosophy, and renewing the Jewish disciplines of study that had been neglected for centuries.

Like most of the founding members of Haskalah, Mendelssohn was self-educated. Born in 1729 to a poor family of distinguished lineage in Dessau, he studied the Talmud—the main writings of Rabbinic Judaism and the primary source of Jewish religious law and theology. He enrolled in a newly established Yeshiva in Berlin in 1743, where he studied Jewish philosophy. With the financial assistance of two medical students, he acquired a secular education in the new Enlightenment sciences.

While in Berlin, Mendelssohn met and became fast friends with Gotthold Ephraim Lessing (1729–1781). The son of a Lutheran minister, Lessing was a writer, a philosopher, a playwright, an art critic, and a prominent representative of the German Enlightenment. His books were among the first to be ceremoniously burned during the rise of Nazism in the 1930s. Their friendship was authentic and full of warmth. For those who knew them, it exemplified the Enlightenment's goal of overcoming religious differences. Mendelssohn's project was the retrieval of biblical wisdom and poetry as a model for European Christian and Jews. For his part, Lessing, as a devoted son of Enlightenment dogma, promoted a "Christianity of reason." He saw no use for biblical revelation. Human reason sharpened by criticism and dissent was sufficient to guide the course of human civilization.

Mendelssohn routinely used biblical equivalents for issues raised by Enlightenment thinkers and raised their horizons from the merely human to the divine. For example, German philosophes, such as Christian Wolff (1679–1754), prompted a renewed interest in the ideal of friendship. Wolff saw friendship as delighting in increasing another's perfection. Mendelssohn introduced the friendship of David and Jonathan to exemplify Wolff's view. Drawing on the Talmudic tradition, Mendelssohn interpreted the Wolffian idea of friendship as unconditional love, which pointed beyond the human to God. From a solely human view, friendship or *philia* may indeed give pleasure in the other's higher perfection. But friendship in the rabbinical tradition pointed to a greater love, the love of God, and since he embodies all perfection, joy results from obedience to his law.

This example is consistent with the Mendelssohn's lifelong project: combining Enlightenment philosophy and the Torah—God's law revealed to Moses and recorded in the first five books of the Bible, the Pentateuch (Genesis, Exodus, Leviticus, Numbers, and Deuteronomy). Without the Torah and the tradition of its interpretation, humankind was "like a blind man in the dark."[4] Not surprisingly, Mendelssohn's most enduring accomplishment was a large-scale Hebrew-to-German translation of the Pentateuch with an accompanying commentary that underlined the Bible as the ultimate source of practical knowledge. Faith, as exemplified by Abraham and Moses, was for Mendelssohn a form of practical knowledge that led to action.

Mendelssohn was of one mind with his Enlightenment conversation partners on the importance of knowledge. He differed by emphasizing practical knowledge over their primary interest in theoretical and abstract knowledge. This emphasis is clear throughout his Pentateuch commentary. He often discussed scientific ideas as they might be relevant to certain biblical passages. But he insisted that an extended formal discussion of scientific theories had no place in explanations of passages such as the Genesis creation story. For they are alien to the essence of Torah and the faith of Jews. For Jews, "Torah is a possession . . . to know the commandments which God has enjoined us to learn and to teach, to observe and to fulfill."[5]

Besides his Pentateuch translations and commentary, Mendelssohn was passionately committed to a translation of the psalms that expressed something about the particular relations between the elite of the German Enlightenment and contemporary Judaism. The psalms were a way for Mendelssohn to draw parallels between the eighteenth-century

Enlightenment and what he termed a *biblical, Jewish Enlightenment*, exemplified by King David, the author of the psalms. At the core of Mendelssohn's Religious Enlightenment project was an affirmation of Judaism as a repository of wisdom and knowledge available to those committed to the secular Enlightenment movement.

Joseph Eybel: Catholic Reformism in Habsburg Austria

Joseph Eybel's Catholic reforms under the Habsburg monarchy somewhat resembled the Haskalah in its retrieval of neglected intellectual traditions, but with a significant difference. Haskalah received no governmental support, but Eybel's reforms had the full and substantial backing of the Habsburg monarchy.

The Thirty Years' War nearly bankrupted the House of Habsburg. But in two generations after its humiliation at the Peace of Westphalia, it assembled a new empire of considerable size and influence. By 1740 it had become one of Europe's great powers, along with France, Russia, and Great Britain. It differed from its rivals in that it was not a nation-state with mainly one dominant ethnicity. With its headquarters in Vienna, Austria, its rule extended over a far-flung and highly diverse collection of states and smaller principalities, running from the southern Netherlands to northern Italy, and the Balkan states to the heartlands of Austria and Bohemia. Although German influence was prevalent, the empire was thoroughly international. Its aristocracy, active both in the Viennese court and in the vast countryside, included Czechs, Hungarians, Italians, Germans, and Croats.

The empire's subjects included innumerable ethnic groups who professed Catholicism, Lutheranism, Calvinism, Judaism, and Eastern Orthodoxy. The Habsburg monarchy sustained its control of these widely varying nationalities and religions through its strong commitment to Catholicism. Its public ceremonies, the glorious splendor of Baroque music art and architecture, an unflagging allegiance to the primacy of papal authority, and its mostly Jesuit-run educational institutions taken together were unabashedly Catholic. Crucially important to the Catholicity of the empire was the Jesuit system of higher education known as the *Ratio Studiorum* (Plan of Study) with its tightly prescribed method of teaching theology, philosophy, and the sciences, combined with the study of great playwrights and authors, such as Sophocles, Euripides, Cicero, Seneca, Dante (especially), Petrarch, and Boccaccio. This plan of study combined the liberal arts education of the Middles Ages with the humanism of the Italian Renaissance of the 1400s.

Eybel was a major influence in transforming the Habsburg's Austrian empire from a regime of Catholic absolutism to Austrian-state absolutism, and from a universal Roman Catholicism to a state Catholicism, or more precisely, a state church. In short, absolute monarchy is a government in which a king or queen holds supreme authority, nearly unbounded by written laws, legislature, or customs.

Eybel succeeded as a Religious Enlightener because he enjoyed the favor of two of the greatest and most powerful eighteenth-century monarchs: the empress Maria Theresa (reigned 1740–1780) and her son, Joseph II (reigned 1780–1790). Both mother and son were reform minded, but son more than mother. They sought ways to strengthen the power and authority of the Austrian monarchy, which were necessary to unify and effectively govern the empire's multiplicity of peoples. Since the empire's identity was indistinguishable from Catholicism, the reforms aimed at increasing and centralizing the power of the empire had to begin with reforming Catholicism. Their aim was to subordinate the Church completely to the power of the throne. Eybel was at the ready to supply the theological, philosophical, and legal groundwork to support these aims. Eybel was a radical reformer, whose programs drew heavily from secular Enlightenment ideas. His end game aligned perfectly with the monarchs he served: the establishment of an Austrian state church.

Born into a middle-class Viennese family during the great resurgence of Habsburg power in the 1740s, Eybel was Jesuit educated. He entered the priesthood in his early twenties but then suddenly turned on his Jesuit teachers and left the priesthood. He continued his education, mastering the emerging fields of economics, political science, and natural law. By way of talent, connection, and opportunity, he maneuvered his way into a position of major influence in the courts of Maria Theresa and Joseph II.

Eybel's contemporaries regarded him as arrogant, brash, and often brutal. While he did not begin the movement to reform Austrian Catholicism, he extended it to its logical conclusions. Reform Catholicism was a reaction against the Catholic Church's first response to the Protestant Revolt of the early 1500s, which took its direction from the decrees of the Council of Trent (1545–1563). With the Jesuits leading the way, the Tridentine (for Trent) program consisted of reviving the writings of St. Thomas Aquinas, solidifying the papacy, expanding Baroque art and architecture, establishing new religious orders and reenergizing existing one, and promoting pilgrimages and public processions.

When Eybel came of age in the 1760s, an Austrian backlash to Tridentine Catholicism was well underway. Its intellectual source was not St. Thomas Aquinas but Enlightenment scientists and philosophers, especially Isaac Newton and Immanuel Kant. Austrian Reform Catholicism rejected the primacy of papal authority in favor of the authority of national councils of bishops and cardinals. It toned down public displays of Catholicism, sought control of Church property, promoted toleration of religious differences, and celebrated sacred liturgies in the vernacular rather than Latin.

Eybel drove these reform measures to extremes, rejecting the Jesuit *Ratio Studiorum* in favor of a system for educating not only good Christians but also good citizens loyal to the Austrian monarchy. As a legal scholar, he sought a return to the Church law of the early centuries before the papacy appropriated it for its own purposes. For centuries, he claimed, the papacy had created a pattern of "lies that destroy[ed] the common welfare,"[6] which resulted in "seven long centuries of continuous, horrible ignorance." The "poison of these principles"[7] was to justify the papacy's unprecedented growth and centralization of power.

Eybel aimed to reverse what he considered to be the papacy's usurpation of power and restore it rightfully to monarchs and bishops: "All aspects of our church law," he wrote, "must necessarily have the stamp of antiquity." Eybel believed that relocating power and authority with bishops and monarchs reconciled religious belief and the public good. Doing so would establish a greater harmony "between a holy priesthood and a holy state government."[8]

Eybel's program for the purification of the Church had much in common with Calvinism and other Protestant sects that sought to tear away from Catholicism doctrines and practices that complicated the simplicity of the early church. They especially targeted devotion to the saints, public processions, and many other norms of piety. Eybel's reforms were a form of primitivism that was deeply suspicious of historical developments in the Church. Besides Eybel's Protestant influences, he took from the secular Enlightenment a belief that reason alone could discern the laws of nature.

To be sure, ideas about the natural law predated the Enlightenment by centuries. The Enlightenment version of natural law claimed that unaided human reason could comprehend a universal moral order because morality and human relations, particularly the central values of the Enlightenment, human freedom, and equality, are present in the nature of things. Secular Enlightenment thinkers insisted that the laws of nature would make themselves clearer as the natural sciences progressed. They believed firmly that the order of inanimate nature would eventually reveal the true moral and political order for human society.

Eybel elevated this enlightenment version of the natural law over Church or canon law, which had prevailed until the regime of Maria Theresa. He rejected Church leaders and the need for revelation to guide human conduct. Enlightenment conceptions of natural law (moral law derived from scientific investigations of the natural world) provided Eybel the grounds for the Austrian state to override the Church's historical role on a range of issues.

For Eybel it was the queen or king's absolute duty to eliminate any practices, "accretions and devotional trivialities" that were "injurious to the state." The sovereign should abolish "irritating retailing and selling of spiritual objects, church ordinances or even loans, unreasonable denials of reasonable dispensations or useful permissions, as well as other abuses" and in addition "to set limits to arbitrary devotions and excessive holidays," including "processions, pilgrimages, brotherhoods."[9] The reduction in the number of holy days also signaled the government's new concern for economic growth. Austrian holy days were days when all work ceased in the empire, thus hampering economic productivity. Eybel also expressed concern that the proliferation of Catholic holy days allowed Protestants to be more productive and wealthier, and thereby better able to support their families and contribute more to their churches.

But the centerpiece of Eybel's Reform Catholicism was providing the legal justification or Joseph II to appropriate the Church's authority over marriage. Marriage law was the fundamental and essential component of the entire Josephist system. For Catholic rulers throughout Europe, gaining control of betrothals, marriages, and annulments was central for maintaining the heredity nature of their rule, stabilizing their governments, making alliances with other powers, and controlling the growth of populations. Eybel argued, "Anytime the sovereign finds it necessary or useful for the state, he can withdraw from the Church the right to determine impediments that destroy the marriage contract." Making his typical appeal to the model of the early church, Eybel argued that "the sovereign has the power and the duty to return, as much as is possible, to the simplicity and purity of the earliest Church discipline."[10] In the case of marriage, Eybel argued that clergy should administer the rites of marriage and the annulment of marriage according to civil, and not canon, law.

Eybel's Reform Catholicism reached its high point during Joseph II's decade of aggressive reform, 1780 to 1790. Had it not been for Joseph, Eybel's reformism would have remained mostly untried. "Without Joseph II, where would I be?"[11] he once asked rhetorically. Following Joseph II's death in 1790, much of Eybel's program collapsed. Joseph's son Francis II (reigned 1792–1835), a conservative, reversed much of Joseph's reforms, in good part because the French Revolution of 1789 cast a dark shadow over the entire Enlightenment. The elements of Reform Catholicism that continued were those that supported the growth of the empire's authority. Thus Eybel had realized the central aim of agenda: the use of religion as a means to advance the power of the sovereign.

The Religious Enlightenment overlapped significantly with the Moderate Enlightenment during the eighteenth century. During that period, the Moderate Enlightenment still had traces of religiosity, which later gave way to a near-total secular view of the world. The fact that the Religious Enlightenment spanned across Protestantism, Catholicism, and Judaism indicates that all religious traditions had to confront the challenges of a new understanding of reason that reduced knowledge to that which could be measured and ascertained with certainty. The Religious Enlightenment decided to engage the Moderate Enlightenment on its territory. In its accommodation to the Moderate Enlightenment it gave great weight to natural religion, which was the home field of the Deists, such as Isaac Newton, and freethinkers such as Thomas Paine. Religious Enlighteners tried to carve out a place for revelation, but they found it increasingly difficult to do so, having ceded so much ground to the Moderate Enlighteners' great preference for reason over revelation. The Religious Enlightenment was short lived, existing as a serious force in the European public sphere for a brief season before its influence petered out entirely.

Up Close and Personal:

ST. MARGARET MARY ALACOQUE (1647–1690)

A full-fledged member of the Enlightenment club, Blaise Pascal dissented from its reduction of the human person to mind alone. He celebrated the heart as the essence of human personhood, not merely as the seat of affection, but as a way of knowing that involved the whole person—intellect, emotions, experience, and intuition. During his night of fire, he found his greatest desire, Jesus. His "Mémorial" testified to this discovery, and he kept it concealed, sewn into his coat, close to his own heart.

Margaret Mary Alacoque was seven years old when the night of fire burned the love and mercy of Christ into Pascal's heart. They were near contemporaries, but it is doubtful that Margaret Mary ever heard of Pascal, let alone his great homage to the human heart. The urbane Pascal moved easily amid the chic socialites of Paris. Margaret Mary was born and raised in a small town in the duchy of Burgundy, which had a rich and storied history but was far removed from the high life of Parisian society. Despite their vast differences in upbringing and celebrity, her devotion to the Sacred Heart of Jesus made clear and unambiguous what Pascal had experienced and kept private—the link between the human heart and the heart of Christ.

Devotion to the Sacred Heart of Jesus predated Margaret Mary, reaching back to the image of St. John the Evangelist resting his head on the Sacred Heart of Jesus. On December 27, 1273, St. John, in a vision, revealed to St. Gertrude the Great

(1256–1302) his special connection to the heart of Jesus. St. Gertrude recorded her dialog with St. John:

> **St. Gertrude:** Well-beloved of the Lord, did these harmonious beatings which rejoice my soul also rejoice thine when thou didst repose during the Last Supper on the bosom of the Savior?
>
> **St. John:** Yes, I heard them, and my soul was penetrated with their sweetness even to its very center.
>
> **St. Gertrude:** Why, then, hast thou spoken so little in thy Gospel of the loving secrets of the Heart of Jesus?
>
> **St. John:** My mission was to write of the Eternal Word . . . but the language of the blissful pulsations of the Sacred Heart is reserved for latter times, that the time-worn world, grown cold in the love of God, may be warmed up by the hearing of such mysteries.[12]

The latter time waited upon the Enlightenment when a grim sort of calculating reason led many hearts to grow cold and, together with the grim doctrines of John Calvin, put God at a great distance from the concerns of humanity. On December 27, 1673, Jesus appeared to St. Margaret Mary and showed her his Sacred Heart, displaying his divine love in the form of flames. He said to her, "My Heart is so full of love for men that It can no longer contain the flames of Its burning love. . . . I must reveal to men and women the treasures of My Heart and save them from perdition."[13]

There is no evidence that St. Margaret Mary had known about the revelation to St. Gertrude or the history of devotion to the Sacred Heart. Her piety was earnest and simple. From a very early age she practiced a deep devotion to the Eucharist and austere mortifications. Her father was a nobleman who lived beyond the family's means. When he died, her mother and six siblings fell on hard times. The family sent Margaret Mary to a convent school run by the Urbanist sisters at Charolles. She enjoyed the ordered, peaceful, and prayer-filled life of the sisters. In her early teens, Margaret suffered a severe case of rheumatic fever, which left her bedridden for four years. She vowed to enter religious life if her disease passed, which it did.

Meanwhile, her family's finances improved, and Margaret returned to her family. At seventeen, her family convinced her that her vow was not binding since she made it as a child. Her mother and brothers then introduced her into Burgundy's social life, with their continuous rounds of dances and balls. They hoped to marry her into a family of some means and social status. Out of obedience, she complied but took no joy in doing so. Following a particularly festive Mardi Gras ball, she had a vision of the scourged and bloodied Christ. He rebuked her for forgetting about him but assured her of his merciful love because she was a child when she made her promise to his mother. Moved by this vision, she recommitted to her childhood vow and, at twenty-four, entered the Visitation Convent at Paray-le-Monial on May 25, 1671.

Over the course of eighteen months beginning on the Feast of St. John in 1673, St. Margaret experienced visions of Jesus in which he asked her to promote a devotion to his merciful heart. Margaret wrote down what Jesus said to her in these visions:

> And He [Christ] showed me that it was His great desire of being loved by men and of withdrawing them from the path of ruin that made Him want to manifest His Heart to men, with all the treasures of love, of mercy, of grace, of sanctification and salvation which it contains, in order that those who desire to render Him and procure Him all the honor and love possible might themselves be abundantly enriched with those divine treasures of which His heart is the source.[14]

Initially, Margaret Mary's mother superior and some theologians denied the veracity of her visions. It was St. Claude de la Colombière, S.J. (1641–1682), her confessor, who in 1683 declared that her visions were authentic. He and his Jesuit confreres then went on to vigorously promote devotion to the Sacred Heart throughout France, and eventually to all of Catholic Europe.

The devotion to the Sacred Heart of Jesus touches the deepest and noblest aspect of the human person. To possess a heart capable of love, one that knows anxiety and sorrow, that is afflicted and moved, is the most indelible mark of human personhood. As St. Margaret Mary knew well, the heart is a person's deepest, most secret center, and it is set afire by the heart of Jesus in which the fullness of divinity lives.

Three centuries after St. Margaret Mary refocused the world on the heart of Jesus, Servant of God Romano Guardini wrote that certainty—the singular quest of the Enlightenment generation and its successors—is the knowledge that "the heart of Jesus Christ is the beginning and end of all things."[15]

Postlude: A Countercultural Community of Spirit

Seventeenth- and eighteenth-century secular and religious Enlightenment leaders, separated and spread out as they were across Europe and America, thought of themselves and their project as united in a virtual "republic of letters." Taken together, St. Margaret Mary and the religious and saints we have discussed thus far, are a counterculture to this "republic": a family of souls, a community of spirit inspired by the spirituality of the Visitation sisters, the Society of Jesus, and the Apostle of Gentleness, St. Francis de Sales.

The founding of the Visitation sisters—the Order of St. Margaret Mary, was a collaboration between St. Jane Frances de Chantal (1572–1641) and St. Francis de Sales. The sickness, poverty, and devastation wrought by the Thirty Years' War weighed heavily on Jane Frances. In response, she set to out to establish an order based on the Blessed Mother's visit to her elderly cousin Elizabeth when she was expecting. The sisters would visit the sick and take in the elderly and infirm into their order. The rigorous austerity of other orders would often be too much for these women, who nonetheless had a religious vocation.

St. Francis de Sales helped write the rule and sponsor the order. It was the mercy of God that led St. Francis to his priestly vocation. As a student he met the severe and grim doctrine of John Calvin, in which the decision for a person's eternal destiny was preordained and unaffected by human effort or prayer. The symbol of the rungless ladder between earth and heaven captured the essence of Calvinism: what appeared to be a way to heaven had no steps to get there. The thought that God might have pre-destined him to eternal damnation drove St. Francis to deep despair. His discovery and deep reflections on Divine Mercy brought him back from the brink.

St. Francis de Sales remained the guardian of St. Jane Frances's order until his death, when St. Vincent de Paul stepped into the role. The spirit of affinity and of heart between St. Francis and St. Vincent was such that St. Jane Frances found no difference in their spiritual guidance.

With these foundations in charity and mercy, the Visitation commu-nity was the perfect setting to bring forth St. Margaret Mary's vision and devotion to the Sacred Heart, and for the reception of Fr. Jean-Pierre de Caussade's doctrine of self-abandonment to Divine Providence. Recall that it was the Visitation sisters who preserved the conferences of Caussade. The nexus of Salesian, Visitation, Vincentian, and Jesuit spiritualities was an assurance of the continued love of God for each person. It provided an unexpected countercurrent to the distant and affectively unavailable God of Isaac Newton and John Calvin.

YOU BE THE JUDGE:

Should you take Pascal's wager?

Games of chance were all the rage in the 1600s. That is in part why Pascal's writing on probability made him so popular among the learned of his time. His famous "logic of the wager" on the fundamental question of God's existence is sometimes mistaken for a proof for the existence of God. Voltaire was among those who made this mistake. As a "proof of God" it was, in Voltaire's view, crude and infantile. But Pascal proposed his wager not as a proof of God's existence but rather as an unavoidable decision, whether made deliberately or not. Declining the bet, he argues, is not an option. "A coin is being spun which will come down heads or tails. How will you wager? Reason cannot make you choose either, reason cannot prove either wrong."[16] That said, however, you can use your reason to make the right wager.

For Pascal the decision of whether to believe in the existence of God is a pragmatic one: what are the consequences of living a life believing in God and, alternatively, living as if there were no God. If God truly exists, and we believe—that is, we wager that God exists—then we have an infinite gain: eternal and infinite beatitude. If God truly exists, and we do not believe that, then we have the potential of an infinite loss: damnation, or at least eternal separation from God, according to Christian teaching.

If there is no God, and we believe God exists, then we lose nothing, and at least have gained a good reputation among others for exhibiting admirable human virtues, such as faithfulness, humility, gratitude, generosity, loyalty, sincerity, and truthfulness.

If God really does not exist, and we believe he does not exist, we essentially gain nothing of enduring worth.

For Pascal it is always more reasonable to bet on an infinite gain—to risk the lesser for the greater. An infinite gain always trumps even a finite loss or gain. Accordingly, it is always more reasonable to wager that God exists. If you bet wisely, you win it all.

Besides Voltaire, Pascal's wager has attracted criticisms from many quarters. To give one example, there is an objection that asks whether belief is really a matter of choice. Some who ask this question argue that it is impossible to adopt a belief simply because we decide to do so. You may take Pascal's advice and bet on God's existence and act accordingly. But that does not mean you have given full assent of mind, heart, and soul to belief in God. To answer this sort of objection, C. S. Lewis says that acting in a certain way—such as having faith in the truth of God's existence—will eventually bring you around to authentic belief.

So, are you a betting person? Is Pascal's wager a good bet? Would you take it?

Chapter 4

The Enlightenment in the Tradition of European Renewal Movements

The Fifth Gospel: A Portrait of J. S. Bach

It was difficult to walk by any of the stunningly beautiful churches of Leipzig and resist stopping in. On a particularly warm, sunny day, a reserved, pious man was passing by the Church of St. Nicholas, unique for its mix of twelfth-century Romanesque and sixteenth-century Gothic elements. The church's architecture complemented perfectly the majestic strains of its newly rebuilt organ, which could be heard from blocks away. Hearing these strains, the passerby felt compelled to get a closer look.

He entered the church and climbed the steps to the choir loft. He listened as the organist played the final section of an intricate fugue. The visitor applauded the organist's playing and asked if he could try out the renovated organ. The organist was delighted to show off the new instrument. The visitor played and the two talked musical shop. Each one demonstrating a point with a musical example on the organ. Gradually, a contest of skill began. Initially, the two organists seemed evenly matched. But after a while, the visitor's explosive creativity and virtuosic playing was on full display, which caused the resident organist of St. Nicholas to suddenly embrace the visitor with great admiration. He exclaimed, you must be an angel of God or Johann Sebastian Bach. The visitor assured his host that he was not an angel.

Such was the reputation of Johann Sebastian Bach (1685–1750). Born into a large Lutheran family in Eisenach, Thuringia, in east-central Germany, he showed keen musical and intellectual talent, especially in music theory, theology, and Latin. His family included fifty-three professional musicians. When Bach's parents died prematurely within nine months of each other, Sebastian's brother Johann Christian took him in. The loss of his parents weighed heavily on him. But the comfort of a large family was a great consolation, an experience that for him was always associated with music. An extended Bach family gathering featured singing and instrumental performances. A family tradition was the "quodlibet" (what-you-like), which consisted of harmonizing and improvising on popular songs of the day, usually with wry and, at times, bawdy musical humor.

In most everything he did musically, Bach combined Enlightenment and pre-Enlightenment ideas and values in nearly equal measure. He moved easily between secular court life and the world of Lutheran liturgy and theology. He was without compromise, an extremely devout and pious Lutheran. In his need to expand the emotional and spiritual registers of his faith, he refashioned classical theories of sound to create a system of tuning that allowed him to heighten the dramatic quality of his music. Illustration 4.1 depicts Bach's "well-tempered" system. It is a circle of fifths (each letter is five steps away from the previous letter or key), which facilitated easier and more interesting ways to move from one tonal center to another. (See illustration 4.1 at https://www.avemariapress.com/church-and-the-age-of-enlightenment-art for an image of J. S. Bach's "well-tempered" system.)

Like Isaac Newton's color wheel (see illustration 2.1), which expanded the pallet of painters, Bach's circle of fifths opened up new expressive possibilities for musicians, but with a fundamental difference. Bach's exploration and use of music theory and acoustics (the physics of sound) was put mainly in the service of widening music's expressiveness to convey more powerfully the Christian faith. The subtle gradations of Bach's well-tempered tuning meant that certain keys sounded slightly different (brighter or darker) than other keys. Consequently, various emotions and moods were ascribed to various keys, which Bach used to great effect in his masterwork, the *St. Matthew Passion*. Its fusion of musical elements, especially the constant movement from key to key, monumental structure, and incessant intertwining of musical lines, animated the text of St. Mathew's gospel such that audiences then and now feel the appalling suffering of Jesus with great force—so much so that a Lutheran archbishop once called Bach's *St. Matthew Passion* "the fifth gospel." (For an excerpt from J. S. Bach's *St. Matthew Passion*, Finale, see musical example 4.1 at https://www.avemariapress.com/church-and-the-age-of-enlightenment-art.)

Besides a demanding schedule of composing and performing, Bach carried a full schedule of students to whom he taught Latin and organ. His love of Cicero's (106–43 BC) elegant Latin informed another of Bach's musical ambitions: to make pure music (music not set to words) more understandable by making it more like speech, a kind of musical rhetoric. Bach's extensive catalog of instrumental compositions demonstrates his success in achieving this aim.

The success of the German Enlightenment owed much to Bach's achievement. The importance of Isaac Newton's mathematized reasoning among German Enlighteners, such as Immanuel Kant, is not at all trivial. But as Christopher Dawson keenly observed, "The German view of life is in fact musical rather than mathematical."[1] Music was always a mathematical discipline, a practical application of the liberal art of arithmetic. But it took Bach's original use of mathematics and acoustical science to intensify the dramatic and emotional power of music and lay the groundwork for a view of life that was indeed musical.

Christianity: The Source of Cultural and Social Renewal

The Enlightenment was a renewal movement, one in a series of renewals in European history. It was a renaissance, or rebirth, of sorts. It is customary to think of renaissance as a reference to the Italian Renaissance of the 1400s and the artistic achievements of Leonardo da Vinci, Michelangelo, and Botticelli, among many others. But in actuality the Italian Renaissance was only one of a series of great European renaissances, or renewal movements, each one inspired by Christianity and producing significant advances in apostolic zeal, theology, philosophy, science, literature, poetry, and the visual arts. Each of these renaissances touched upon all that was fully human—heart, mind, and soul. Most important, they extended and strengthened Europe's spiritual unity.

What unified the diversity of European peoples for more than a millennium was a religious tradition, Christianity, which shaped its essential beliefs, ideals, culture, and institutions. The Enlightenment, which was nominally Christian at least in its moderate form, shattered this unity. As noted in chapter 2, for Enlighteners of all kinds, the mind alone was the source of meaning and value. Mind was everything, but it was disembodied mind. To be sure, the Enlightenment and the tradition of mathematical reason and experiential science it promoted succeeded in making earthly life materially a little better for more and more people. But it did not possess the social and cultural dynamism of earlier European renewal movements. What follows is a brief survey of Europe's major renewal movements (renaissances) and their achievements.

The Anglo-Irish Renaissance (650–750)

The Anglo-Irish or Northumbrian Renaissance began shortly after the Gregorian mission of AD 597, when St. Gregory the Great sent St.

Augustine of Canterbury and more than forty Italian monks and priests to evangelize England. Despite initial native resistance to the Gospel, and the constant threat of Viking invasions, the monks managed to establish a series of monasteries, which became centers of evangelization and original cultural achievements.

Eadfrith, the bishop of Lindisfarne, just off the coast of Northumbria, created the famous Lindisfarne Gospels, a magnificently illuminated manuscript of the four gospels probably produced around AD 715. Eadfrith wrote and illustrated them in honor of St. Cuthbert, who preceded Eadfrith as bishop of Lindisfarne. Eadfrith richly adorned the gospels and encased them in a finely crafted leather binding bedecked with jewels. Its illuminative art combined elements of early Roman and Irish-Anglo artists styles.

Included in the Northumbrian Renaissance was the work of St. Bede (672–735), the most learned scholar of his age and a Doctor of the Church. His contributions ranged widely, encompassing history, theology, science, and literature. His most famous work was the *Ecclesiastical History of the English People*, which set the standard for historical writing and earned him the title of the Father of English History. Bede was also a pioneer in the science of *computus*—the basis for building calendars. Bede undertook this work to determine the exact date for Easter each year, a tradition that had been lost during the Roman persecutions of Christians. He also standardized the practice of dating forward from the birth of Christ (*Anno Domini*—in the year of our Lord).

The literary jewel of the Anglo-Irish Renaissance was *Beowulf*. Written in the late 600s, it is a foundational work in English poetry. The poem had lost its place among the great works of world literature until J. R. R. Tolkien restored it to prominence. In his famous 1936 lecture "*Beowulf*: The Monsters and the Critics," Tolkien saw Grendel, the work's chillingly frightful monster, and the unnamed dragon in the poem as enemies of Christ. Tolkien's essay explored the interplay between pre-Christian, pagan thought and myth with Christianity, which the anonymous author of *Beowulf* fused brilliantly. The influence of *Beowulf* on Tolkien's *Hobbit* and *Lord of the Rings* is difficult to miss.

The Carolingian Renaissance (800–950)

In AD 800 on Christmas Day in Rome, Pope Leo III crowned Charlemagne (Charles the Great) the first western European Holy Roman Emperor. Charlemagne became the standard for imperial legitimacy until Napoleon ended the institution of the Holy Roman Emperor in 1806. Charlemagne held more territory in western Europe than any man since the Caesars of the Roman Empire. His lands extended from the Atlantic to Vienna and from northern Germany to Rome.

His Carolingian Renaissance was a period of extraordinary cultural and literary achievement. Its centerpiece was the Benedictine monasteries that had been founded throughout Europe. His alliance with the monastic culture enabled Charlemagne and his son, Louis the Pious, to achieve their ambitious plans to reform the Church's government, elevate the education of the clergy, and unify liturgical practices.

The monasteries were amazingly resilient institutions. During the period of the Carolingian Renaissance, western Europe was continually besieged by Vikings from the north, Magyars from the east, and Islam from the south and west. Nonetheless, ninety-nine out of a hundred monasteries could be destroyed and leveled, and from the one remaining, the whole Benedictine rule, liturgy, and storehouse of learning could be reconstituted in less than a generation.

Although the political structure of Charlemagne's empire lasted less than a century, the cultural and religious unity it achieved established the foundation for all later intellectual and cultural developments of the European Middle Ages. The Carolingian Renaissance also had links to the Northumbrian Renaissance through the Anglo-Saxon missionary St. Boniface (675–754) and Alcuin of York (ca. 735–804). Charlemagne was an enthusiastic promoter of science, theology, and the arts, assembling at his court the most learned men from every part of Europe. Few sovereigns had a clearer sense of the importance of education and a greater concern for cultivating literature and the arts. His court was characterized by regular discussions among nobles, scholars, and laymen on faith, reason, science, poetry, and the visual arts.

The Carolingian Renaissance exhibited the first sustained interest in a Christian Humanism and a Christian culture. Alcuin, whom Charlemagne recruited from Northumbria, was the intellectual north star of Charlemagne's Renaissance and led the way for Carolingian scholars to preserve and advance the study of mathematics, philosophy, theology, poetry, and theories of education (pedagogy). Alcuin was enthusiastic for Charlemagne's vision. He once wrote to Charlemagne that if Charlemagne realized his plan of renewal,

> it may be that a new Athens will arise in France, and an Athens fairer than of old, for our Athens informed by the teachings of Christ, will surpass the wisdom of the [Athenian] Academy. The old Athens had only the teachings of Plato to instruct it, yet even so it flourished by the seven liberal arts. But our Athens will be enriched by the sevenfold gift of the Holy spirit and will, therefore, surpass all the dignity of earthly wisdom.[2]

Alcuin's reference to the seven liberal arts here is important. From antiquity through 1400, the curriculum of higher education included seven subjects: grammar, rhetoric, and logic (called the *trivium*), and arithmetic, music, geometry, and astronomy (the *quadrivium*). The trivium studied the arts of language; the quadrivium, the arts of measure. Arithmetic was the theory of number; music, or more precisely music theory, its application. Geometry was the theory of space; astronomy, its application. The trivium and quadrivium formed a unity of the literary and the mathematical, a unity that the Enlightenment undermined with its total commitment to mathematics as the medium for all reasoning, learning, and societal progress.

The Ottonian Renaissance (950–1050)

The Ottonian Renaissance of the tenth and eleventh centuries takes its name from the three emperors of the Saxon dynasty, Otto I (reigned 936–973), Otto II (reigned 973–983), and Otto III (reigned 983–1002). Their empire succeeded Charlemagne's as the great power of Europe during the tenth and eleventh centuries. Their lands extended from Rome on the south to the North Sea, and from France on the west to Poland and Hungary on the east. Whereas the Northumbrian and Carolingian renaissances blended the indigenous cultures of England, Ireland, and northern Europe with Roman, Greek, and Christian influences. The Ottonian Renaissance combined many elements of Byzantium (Eastern Christianity) with western European Latin cultures. The reign of the three Ottos was also the high-water mark of collaboration between the papacy and the territories of northern Europe. As noted earlier, this unity was undone by the Treaty of Westphalia and the reforms of Joseph Eybel and Emperor Joseph II during the Religious Enlightenment.

Like the Carolingian Renaissance, the achievements of the Ottonian Renaissance ranged across the arts and sciences. Architecture, metalworking, painting, and sculpture were especially reinvigorated by the Ottos' renewed contact with Constantinople, the capitol of the Eastern Roman Empire. The Ottos also rebuilt and strengthened the network of cathedral schools throughout their empire. These schools were centers of advanced learning, some of which became the universities in the later Middles Ages. Their curriculum was the seven liberal arts. Teachers were selected for their love of learning and love of God. Students were preparing either for Holy Orders or for administrative positions in the courts of Europe.

Among the most fascinating figures of the late Ottonian Renaissance was Hermanus Augiensis, also known as Hermanus Contractus

(1013–1054). He was a mathematician, a historian, a musician, and a poet. The son of a prominent nobleman, Hermanus suffered from a severe birth defect that nearly immobilized him. With an iron will he overcame his disability and with great difficulty learned to read and write. At the age of seven, his father recognized his son's amazing intellectual abilities and placed him under the care of one of Germany's most learned abbots. Hermanus loved the monastic life and took the vows of the Benedictine order in 1043. He quickly became famous for his wide learning in mathematics, theology, astronomy, music, Latin, Greek, and Arabic. He attracted students from all over Europe and the Byzantine Empire not only for his intellect but also for his life of holiness and his affable personality.

Hermanus wrote treatises on mathematics and astronomy, and most notably a chronicle of the major historical events between the time of Christ to the eleventh century. His is the earliest of the medieval universal chronicles still in existence. Like St. Bede, his history was impeccably well sourced, elegantly written, and accurate. Many of his sources came to him though oral tradition. In the field of music, he built musical instruments and composed many religious hymns. He is most probably the author of two famous Marian hymns: *Alma Redemptoris Mater* (Loving Mother of Our Savior) and *Salve Regina* (Hail Holy Queen). These hymns continue in use in the Night Prayer of the Church (Compline) to this day. (To listen to *Salve Regina* and *Alma Redemptoris Mater* by Hermann Contractus, also known as Hermann of Reichenau, see musical examples 4.2 and 4.3 at https://www.avemariapress.com/church-and-the-age-of-enlightenment-art.)

The Twelfth-Century Renaissance

The intellectual, artistic, and cultural achievements of the twelfth century matched and exceeded the previous renaissances. But the advances in science were the hallmark of this renaissance. To be sure, the scientific advances of the Enlightenment outpaced those of the twelfth-century renaissance. But the significant difference is that the twelfth-century scientific advances were part of a web of intellectual renewals in theology, philosophy, the arts, and literature, whereas in the Enlightenment scientific development was cut off from theological and Christian humanistic contexts.

An important aspect of each of the European renaissances was the integration of the learning, literature, and art of different cultures, unified by the Christian tradition. The Northumbrian and Carolingian renaissances fused Greek, Roman, and Nordic cultures. The Ottonian combined western European, Latin culture with that of eastern, Byzantine Christian culture. The twelfth century introduced the Arabic recovery of ancient Greek writings, especially those of Aristotle (368–348 BC), which had been lost to western Europe with the fall of the Roman Empire in the fifth century.

The twelfth century made systematic advances in each of the major branches of theoretical and applied sciences: mathematics, geometry, astronomy, physics, geography, medicine, veterinary medicine, botany, engineering, and architecture. Experimental science, which was held in the highest esteem during the Enlightenment, had its precursor in the 1100s. Chief among the great experimental scientists was the Universal Doctor of the Church, St. Albert the Great (1199–1280), teacher of St. Thomas Aquinas.

Twelfth-century scholars were flush with excitement over the rediscovery and retrieval of Aristotle's writing through Europe's contact with the Arab world. Few works of Aristotle survived the collapse of the Roman Empire in the Latin West. Eastern Christians preserved all of Aristotle's works, and when they made contact with the Muslim world, most of Aristotle's body of writing was translated into Arabic from 750 to 1000. They then found their way into the Latin West in Arabic, which were then translated into Latin.

Aristotle's stature was so great that men of the twelfth century referred to him merely as "The Philosopher." St. Albert had access to the whole of Aristotle's writings. He commented on them extensively. But he did not take everything Aristotle said at face value. He insisted on observation and experimentation to validate what Aristotle had set forth. St. Albert wrote, "The aim of natural science is not simply to accept the statements [*narrata*] of others, but to investigate the causes that are at work in nature."[3] Such a statement could have been written by any one of a number of Enlightenment scientists or philosophers.

There were many other examples of experimental scientific activity. Walcher of Malvern fixed the difference of time between England and Italy from an eclipse. At significant personal risk, Aristippul, another twelfth-century scientist, studied close-up an eruption of Etna. Giraldus Cambrensis recorded the height of the tide in Ireland and Wales, and Michael Scot observed and described the volcanic phenomena of the Lipari Islands. These examples may seem trivial, but they indicate that the sciences, theoretical and experimental, attracted the great minds of pre-Enlightenment Christian Europe with strong support from European sovereigns and the Church. Most important, they enjoyed a free, easy, and friendly exchange with theology, philosophy, art, and literature, an exchange that the Enlightenment project mostly abandoned.

The Italian Renaissance (1400–1600)

Our quick survey of European renaissances now brings us to the fifteenth-century Italian Renaissance, which is almost always identified as *the* Renaissance. Like the Haskalah of the eighteenth century, the Italian Renaissance did not benefit from royal patronage or governmental funding. Its great benefactors were the wealthy members of the Medici family of Florence and, particularly, Lorenzo de' Medici (1449–1492). The Medicis used their wealth to promote beauty, truth, and wisdom, first for the citizens of Florence and then for the rest of the world. In total, from the

1430s to the 1470s, they spent the equivalent of half a billion US dollars in support of education and the visual arts. They funded scholars to search the monastery libraries of Europe for ancient manuscripts that had been thought lost. Philosophers such as Fr. Marsilio Ficino (1433–1499), Angelo Poliziano (1454–1494), and Giovanni Pico (1463–1494) undertook new research into Greek and Roman philosophy. Most notably, they brought forward the philosophy of Plato (ca. 428–348 BC) and harmonized it with Christianity.

Lorenzo's greatest energy went into commissioning works of art, which he saw as tightly connected to the realm of ideas and indispensable for a flourishing civil society. For that reason, he stayed closely involved with those he supported. For example, Michelangelo (1475–1564) lived with Lorenzo and his family for five years, joining their family dinners and participating in discussions led by Fr. Ficino, the intellectual father of the Italian Renaissance. The Medicis had a vision, a mission for the arts and for philosophy, and were clear and firm in putting it forward. They wanted to put painting in the service of ideas and to make these ideas palpable, effective, and life changing.

The Italian Renaissance was constantly promoting philosophy, not as an academic discipline, but as a prompt for people to think. Then as now philosophers were thought to inhabit an abstract realm removed from most people's workaday concerns. So, Raphael, one of the great painters of all time, infused philosophy with life. His paintings on the walls of the Vatican show Aristotle and Plato and others as belonging to a group of attractive, fascinating people.

Guided by Fr. Ficino, the Medicis viewed the visual arts as a means of educating the citizens of the Italian city-states. Ficino entered the priesthood in 1477 and served out his apostolate at the cathedral of Florence. Ficino reintroduced the works of Plato into Renaissance Italy. Based on his reading of Plato's works and the Christian gospels, Ficino insisted that love was the essence of what it meant to be human, and love is attracted first to beauty. During his dinners at the Medicis and other gatherings he encouraged artists to exemplify essential philosophical and theological truths and virtues, such as civic friendship and generosity. He expected art to encourage serenity and civil peace, and to glorify the best qualities of leadership.

Although philosophy and ideas fascinated the leaders of the Italian Renaissance, they were nevertheless relentlessly practical. Above all else, they wanted to govern their societies successfully, to make their people wise. Thus they built magnificent cities to make them so. They ransacked the past in order to create better ways of thinking and acting in the present. The architecture of public buildings and plazas, fountains, cathedrals, and churches in Florence, Siena, Venice, Pisa, Mantua, and Rome evidence an unrivaled attention to beauty—beauty in the service of a philosophical mission. The patrons, architects, and civil engineers of the Italian Renaissance built their cities with one idea in mind: that residents of cities are to a large extent shaped by the character of the buildings around them. They made sure the public realm conveyed dignity and calm. These qualities helped to ensure the tranquility, vigor, and happiness of all, such that the wealthy in society would not be tempted to withdraw into private enclaves to avoid public squalor. The goal was to create a public sphere that was hospitable to all classes. Such was the Italian Renaissance vision of communal life.

In this whirlwind of intellectual and artistic creation, Christianity remained centrally important. For example, in 1488 Giovanni Bellini (1430–1516) completed a triptych for the Basilica di Santa Maria Gloriosa dei Frari in Venice, featuring in the central panel Mary and the infant Jesus. Artists had been painting this scene for many centuries. Before Bellini's painting, Mary and her baby appeared stiff and wooden. But with Bellini, Jesus looks like a real little boy, down to his stocky legs, slightly swollen tummy, and searching eyes. Mary feels equally alive, vibrant, and deeply attractive and interesting. The painting suggests her melancholy thoughts, those that she pondered in her heart. We intuit her kind, sympathetic, and dignified nature. (See illustration 4.2, Giovanni Bellini's Frari Triptych at https://www.avemariapress.com/ church-and-the-age-of-enlightenment-art.)

The Italian Renaissance was a unique collaboration of visionary philanthropy, Christianity, philosophy, and artists to express and promote truth, goodness, and beauty—the great transcendentals that are found in God and that lead people to God. The Italian Renaissance exemplified a mission-driven coherence that has never been duplicated.

It is not uncommon for some historians to see the Italian Renaissance as the root of the Enlightenment because of its great focus on learning and the development of a certain kind of humanism. But the connection between the two movements is unsustainable for mainly four reasons. First, the Renaissance had a comprehensive idea of the common good, which was more than a concern for material comfort. The great public art of the Renaissance was attentive to the human form, but not for its own sake. It pointed people to a higher, transcendent reality. Second, the culture of the Renaissance city-states was deliberate in unifying all social classes. The Enlightenment tended to isolate society's elites from other classes. This withdrawal bred a certain, and at times palpable, disdain for nonelites.

A third difference is the unbreakable link between science and the humanities celebrated by the men and women of the Renaissance, a link severed by Enlighteners' single-minded commitment to rationalism and the mind as the sole source of societal renewal. Finally, the Renaissance was committed to the integration of Christianity and classic learning and values, whereas the Enlightenment eventually jettisoned Christianity as outmoded and even dangerous to the new order of rationalism.

The Protestant Reformation

Like the Enlightenment, the Protestant Reformation of the sixteenth century is typically not thought of as a renaissance. Nevertheless, it was, like the Enlightenment, a renewal movement of enormous, and even revolutionary, consequence. The sequence of events it set in motion align with the definition of a revolution—the violent transfer of power and property in the service of an idea or ideology. To think of the Protestant Reformation as merely a religious event, a civil war about Christian beliefs, is inaccurate. Its effects went well beyond the sphere of religion. It laid the groundwork for the Enlightenment's celebration of diversity of faith and opinion and encouraged new feelings of nationhood over against a united Christian Europe. In so doing, it deprived Europeans of their ancestral sense of unity and common origins. It elevated the importance of work, changed attitudes toward the arts and human failings, and raised the prestige of vernacular languages to support the emerging nationalism.

But even with the rise of these divisive elements, Europeans and Americans remained united by Christianity. In part, the Catholic-Protestant breach in Christianity occurred precisely because both sides valued the Christian tradition above all else. When Martin Luther (1483–1546), an Augustinian monk and professor of theology, posted his Ninety-Five Theses (or disputed questions) on the door of Wittenberg Cathedral in 1517, he did not intend to prompt a revolt against the Catholic Church. Luther was following a centuries-old practice of probing theological questions by means of an orderly, intellectually rigorous public debate.

A man consumed with the problems of sin, redemption, and salvation, Luther's main interest was "to elicit the truth about the sacrament of penance."[4] The question became explosive in the context of the Church's sale of indulgences—the Church's power to mitigate or eliminate the temporal punishment in eternity associated with a person's sins. This power flows from the Passion, Death, and Resurrection of Christ and the storehouse of merit accumulated by the saints.

Like innumerable debates before 1517, Luther's questions would have most likely remained within a close circle of learned theologians and clerics had it not been for the invention of the printing press, the associated technologies of improved papermaking and ink, and a new group of experienced craftsmen, whose expertise launched a media revolution.

During the Protestant revolt, towns in northern and eastern Germany had multiple firms working twelve-hour shifts, their couriers delivering batches of pamphlets concealed under cloaks to safe distributors—the first underground presses. As in previous renaissances, the arts were pivotal to the Protestant Reformation. Lucas Cranach (1472–1553), Albrecht Dürer (1471–1528), and other famous illustrators provided woodcuts to accompany Protestant tracts, which helped engage those who could not read. Once attracted, people who could read then read them to those who could not read.

The Protestant Reformation was similar to earlier renewal movements in its discovery and retrieval of writings, ideas, and practices that had been forgotten or had fallen into disuse. But its look to the past was extreme, anachronistic in fact, exhibiting a kind of primitivism that sought to purify the Church by leaping back over centuries to an idealized simplicity of apostolic times. It was a desire to slough off what seemed to be the gratuitously complex organization, doctrines, and liturgical practices of the Roman Catholic Church. In anticipation of eighteenth-century Religious Enlighteners, such as Joseph Eybel, the Protestant reformers believed that simple, early Christians, whose only Church authorities were elected overseers, needed only the Gospel, and so it should now also be.

Perhaps Luther did not intend to set off a revolution, but as his controversy with the Vatican escalated, it eventually reached a point of no return. Luther publicly burned Pope Leo X's papal bull condemning forty-one of his Ninety-Five Theses, which delighted the university students who had gathered around Luther. He also threw into the flames books that he disliked for their defense of the papacy and the Roman Church. Watching the conflagration with some glee, Luther said, "It's an old custom to burn bad books."[5]

The Musical Enlightenment

In this brief survey of European renewal movements or renaissances, education, literature, and the visual arts inspired by Christianity were central to the revival and flourishing of societies that were stagnant or had recently experienced some sort of significant disruption. The Enlightenment, as a renewal movement, also had the help of the arts, principally music. The literature, poetry, and painting of the Enlightenment did not rise to the level of creative genius as in previous renewals. But music excelled, thanks in large part to the composer Wolfgang Amadeus Mozart (1756–1791), one of the most influential figures of the Enlightenment. Like Bach, he composed sacred and secular music. Bach was a man with one foot in the Enlightenment and the other in the past. He used the science and art of sound to advance Christianity. Mozart, on the other hand, composed achingly beautiful sacred Masses, but leaned into the secularizing forces of the Enlightenment.

At first it may be startling to include Mozart in a movement that is principally concerned with ideas. But the Enlightenment was a musical culture, a reality that is often overlooked in discussions of the period. For the *philosophes* and the educated public of the Enlightenment, music was not merely entertainment. It was a pleasurable medium to communicate serious new conceptions of society. Enlighteners knew well that music rendered language, ideas, and sentiments more accessible, memorable, and moving.

This view was aided by an important cultural shift in the seventeenth century. The Catholic Mass and other musical settings of scriptural texts moved from the context of liturgical worship to the concert hall. This movement marked a break in the traditional relation between scripture (the word) and belief. In a liturgical event set in a sacred space, music and words combine to form a privileged way of communicating with God. During the Mass or the Divine Offices, the experience of singing, chanting, or hearing scripture set to music is in tune with the very ground of the world's existence, God. St. Augustine of Hippo expressed it simply: "Singing belongs to the one who loves."[6]

Augustine also acknowledged that liturgical music had a double, ambiguous effect, both religious and aesthetic. He wrote in his *Confessions*, "When [I am] more moved by the singing than by what is sung, I confess myself to have sinned criminally, and then I would rather not have heard the singing."[7]

The Enlightenment capitalized on this ambiguity. To be sure, a listener in a concert hall or the intimate space of a salon or café could still experience the sacred music of Bach or Mozart as an expression of Christian belief. But that experience is more ambiguous in these nonsacred spaces. It is principally an aesthetical experience in which the listener is moved by the beauty of the music. This ambiguity in the experience of music was the key to how the Enlightenment used music to gradually move its hearers from an experience of music directed primarily to God to one associated with earthly, material progress driven by the power of human reason.

For example, Bach, who straddled the pre-Enlightenment and Enlightenment eras, composed music for secular concert halls, but Lutherans heard his sacred music, almost without exception, in their churches. Emphatically, for Bach, music, especially harmony, was a metaphor for God. In the words of the great German writer and stateman Johann Wolfgang von Goethe (1749–1832), "It [Bach's music] is as if the eternal harmony were conversing within itself, as it may have done in the bosom of God just before the creation of the world."[8]

A composer, such as Mozart, accelerated the process by which music went from being a metaphor for God to God himself being a metaphor. In this respect, Mozart's music helped promote Immanuel Kant's "religion within the limits of reason alone." This new religion jettisoned a personal God, the Fall, Redemption, and Christ himself. What remained was God as the regulator of reason—a symbol or metaphor beyond the limits of human reasoning.

Mozart's genius, impishness, and disdain for convention are well known. A famous child prodigy, his father, Leopold, dragged him around the courts of Europe as something like a circus act. Wolfgang's gifts were indeed extraordinary. He could listen to a musical work of just about any length and immediately after hearing it play it from memory or transcribe it. Wolfgang Mozart amassed an enormous body of compositions for choir, string quartets, keyboard, singers, and symphony orchestras. But above all, he loved to compose operas. He composed twenty-two operas using German, Italian, and even Latin texts. Among his most famous operas was *The Magic Flute*, which presented the ideas and values of the Enlightenment in an entirely entertaining way.

The Magic Flute appealed to men and women of high and low culture. It combined the new interest in Egyptian mystery cults and the Masonic religion of humanity. The story is set in an imaginary realm between the sun and the moon. The audience enters the story in the middle of its action. Prince Tamino, assisted by the bird catcher and outrageously comical Papageno—the first antihero in European literature, embark on a rescue mission to save Pamina, the girl Tamino loves and daughter of the Queen of the Night. (See illustration 4.3, a statue of Papageno in front of the City Theatre of Brugge, at https://www.avemariapress.com/church-and-the-age-of-enlightenment-art.)

Three mysterious ladies in the service of the queen provide Tamino with a magic flute and Papageno with magic bells for protection against the forces of evil. Pamina's kidnapper was Sarastro, "a powerful, evil demon," who imprisoned her in his castle. The mission comes to ruin as Monostatos, head of Sarastro's security service, discovers and arrests Tamino and Papageno, and takes Pamina for himself.

As it turns out, Sarastro is not a nefarious tyrant but a benevolent ruler and high priest in the temple of wisdom run by priests of Osiris and Isis. Sarastro learns about Monostatos's prisoners and his lecherous desire for Pamina, for which he soundly rebukes him. Unchastened, Monostatos later spies on Pamina asleep in a garden. A sudden appearance of the Queen of the Night forces him into hiding. In an aria full of rage, the queen gives her daughter a dagger with orders to assassinate Sarastro.

Meanwhile, at Sarastro's orders, Tamino must undergo a series of wisdom trials arranged by the temple priest to prove himself worthy of marrying Pamina. Monostatos and the queen find common cause in upending Sarastro's designs. He joins the queen's plot to destroy the temple in exchange for having her daughter, Pamina. But the conspiracy fails, and the two are magically cast out into eternal night. Sarastro announces the sun's triumph over the night, and with it the dawn of a new era of wisdom and fraternity.

The opera is an unsubtle celebration of the Enlightenment and the creed of freemasonry. Freemasons were originally a medieval craft guild. During the Enlightenment they remade themselves into a fraternal order with an ambitious social and political agenda. Freemasonry included thinkers, painters, musicians, writers, and politicians committed to furthering the ideals of the Enlightenment. They were Deists of a special kind, enamored of ritual and myths that they read as actual history. They reverenced God solely as the great designer of the universe and adopted virtues and practices they attributed to builders, stonemasons, as far back as Egypt. The Catholic Church condemned freemasonry. Pope Clement XII in 1738, Pope Leo XIII in 1890, and the 1917 Code of Canon Law explicitly declared freemasonry a heresy for which its followers were automatically excommunicated.

The marks of freemasonry are on full display in *The Magic Flute*: the imaginary celestial setting (between the moon and the sun), the elaborate rituals in the temple of wisdom, priests in the service of Isis and Osiris, and the mythic contest between darkness and light. Music itself is the great hero of the opera. The magic flute given to Tamino subdues the forces of water and fire that threaten Tamino during his wisdom trials. But, on a larger scale, the music of the opera itself parallels the opera's interest in the liberation from the darkness of the past to the new light of reason. Act 2 opens with a solemn procession of temple priests accompanied by music that is beautifully light and airy, signifying the new light of the Enlightenment. The harmonic movement of the opera moves from the darkness of minor keys to the brightness of major keys. But most important, Mozart revived a classical idea, personified in the myth of Orpheus, that music had the power to wrest life from the grip of death and darkness. Allegorically, this power of music paralleled the Enlightenment's optimistic belief that the world can be remade. In the final words of acts 1 and 2 of *The Magic Flute*, the new world will be "a realm of heaven," where mortals are "equal to gods." (To listen to "March of the Priests" from Mozart's *Magic Flute*, see musical example 4.4 at https://www.avemariapress.com/church-and-the-age-of-enlightenment-art. The priest here refers to the priest of the Temple of Zoroaster.)

Up Close and Personal:

QUEEN CHRISTINA OF SWEDEN (1626–1689)

Chief among the great salon women of Rome during the late 1600s was the extraordinary Christina of Sweden, the daughter of Gustavus Adolphus, the Protestant hero of the Thirty Years' War. She organized the Italian version of the French salon, *conversazioni* (conversations), which expanded to include elaborate dinners, balls, small-scale operas, ballets, and plays. In attendance at these events were Roman nobility, popes, cardinals, bishops, priests, artists, musicians, and leading international scholars and scientists. She was the du Châtelet of her era and much, much more.

When her father died in battle, she was eighteen and suddenly heir to a European great power. Raised Lutheran, she practiced a kind of Christian stoicism but was never settled in her belief. At birth she was taken for a boy because her whole body was covered in hair. Masculine in appearance, she cultivated a mannish demeanor her whole life. Her education was the envy of most men of her time. René Descartes was among the many leading philosophers and scientists whom her father hired to tutor her. She was fluent in Latin, German, English, Italian, Spanish, and her native Swedish. Pascal admired her beyond measure. In a long letter of praise, he dedicated his first calculating machine to her.

Under the influence of the Jesuits, she became more and more interested in Roman Catholicism. But for reasons of state, she could not convert. Like Elizabeth I of England (reigned 1558–1603), she refused to marry, which made her increasing unpopular in Sweden and the courts of Europe. The mounting criticism against her, together with her strong attraction to the Catholic faith, led her to abdicate at the age of twenty-eight and leave the crown to her cousin, Charles Gustavus. In November 1655 in Innsbruck, Austria, she made her public entrance into the Catholic Church. A month later she arrived in Rome, which Pope Alexander VII (reigned 1655–1667) had decorated in her honor. Alexander greeted her personally and administered the sacrament of Confirmation, adding Alexandra to her name.

In Rome, she read theology voraciously and set the standard for involved patronage of the arts and sciences in a manner that recalled the Medicis of Florence. Besides hosting *conversazioni*, she studied voice and commissioned new music from Arcangelo Corelli (1653–1713) and Alessandro Scarlatti (1660–1725), her composers in residence. She organized archeological excavations, established three academies for the arts and sciences, an observatory, a distillery, and an illustrated a book on contemporary problems in chemistry. Christina also remained active in affairs of state. Aiming to prevent the rise of another Cardinal Richelieu in France, Christina persistently petitioned Cardinal Jules Mazarin (1602–1661), chief minister to Louis XIII and Louis XIV of France, for policies favorable to the papacy.

This broad sweep of her achievements and interests does not do justice to the many details of her projects, which are nothing short of breathtaking. Full of Enlightenment zeal for knowledge, she unified her projects by her love of Catholicism. She once said that "the world is threatened with peace and quiet. I love storm, and dread it when the wind abates."[9] Such a threat was unknown to the world her father knew. But it was pretty much the case in post-Westphalia Europe. So, finding no storm, she decided to become one herself, a whirlwind of creative activity, a veritable force of nature.

The Enlightenment's Salon and Café Life

The success of *The Magic Flute* during Mozart's life rested in part in its use of vernacular language—German. The prevailing language for opera was Italian. Of Mozart's twenty-two operas, eight of them were in German, which, because of his compositional genius, firmly established the prestige of German opera. The growing preference for using vernacular language was not only a feature of opera; it was especially significant for disseminating Enlightenment scientific ideas and its new social mores. The wider use of national languages, accompanied by technological advances in printing and heightened interest in the scientific and medical advances, spurred a proliferation of learned and other new, ostensibly secret societies. The

Freemasons were one such society. There were others as well, such as the Rosicrucians (for their rose-cross emblem) and the Illuminati (enlightened), which claimed, falsely, to have recovered lost ancient lineages of men devoted to scientific reasoning. Both were obsessed with the occult and fiercely anti-Christian.

In many towns—not just European capitals—academies formed in which learned persons mingled with those eager to hear about their learning. Such socializing between those of high learning and those eager to learn was extremely rare before the seventeenth century, in large part because the language of the learned had been Latin, which aside from churchmen and the highly educated, few people knew. The new societies included nobility and the burgeoning middle class. They sponsored seminars, presentations, and discussions on the latest discoveries and theories—all outside the purvey of universities, which in the twenty-first century have a near monopoly on these activities. Often, these societies offered cash prizes for answers to disputed questions, the winners earning immediate fame. Such was the case of Jean-Jacques Rousseau, whom we will meet in the next chapter.

Alongside these societies were the many salons presided over by learned women, such as Madame Sainctot, who introduced Blaise Pascal into salon life. Salon ladies directed discussions, networked with internationally renowned figures, and, like Sainctot, promoted gifted up-and-comers. Although French salons were the most famous, they were prevalent all over Europe and in American cities, such as New York, Boston, Charleston, and Philadelphia. An invitation to a salon was highly coveted. To be seen and mingle with the chic, smart set was a sign of one's elevated social status. Acquired learning was a way to rise socially, a pathway to the upper crust, which before the Enlightenment had been mostly unavailable to those without noble rank. Less selective than salons were the new cafés, where the like-minded met to discuss new ideas. The

Parisian café Procope was easily the most well known. There, Denis Diderot and his followers gathered regularly.

The salons gave enduring fame to many women. Sainctot was just one of them. The high intellectual caliber and cultural sophistication of salon women were outstanding by any measure. Most notably, such women as Émilie du Châtelet (1706–1749) set a high bar for European and American salon women. She translated and wrote a commentary on Isaac Newton's *Philosophiae Naturalis Principia Mathematica* (1687), which contained the basic laws of physics. Her translation endures to this day as the standard French version of this pivotal Enlightenment book. Her commentary on it included a significant addition to Newton's theory of energy. A close, lifelong friend of Voltaire, du Châtelet influenced his thinking on a range of questions. She had met Voltaire at one of her father's salons, after which they corresponded and collaborated on a number of scientific and other projects.

The variety of topics discussed at Enlightenment salons and cafés was expansive, especially in the natural sciences. The manner in which they reverenced the new experimental sciences made Deism, and eventually atheism, plausible options as guides for living. Salon and café life helped inch Europe and America toward the secularism that would eventually dominate their societies.

YOU BE THE JUDGE:

Are the arts mirrors or shapers of society?

As we noted earlier, the arts are often considered mirrors of society, reflecting its beliefs, morals, politics, and intellectual trends. Human struggles, discoveries, wars, and much else of significance to men and women have a dramatic influence on art's form and content. As we saw in an earlier chapter, Peter Paul Rubens's *Consequences of War*, 1637–1638, responds to and documents human sufferings. (See illustration 1.2 for an image of *Consequences of War* at https://www.avemariapress.com/church-and-the-age-of-enlightenment-art.) Another iconic painting of war and human suffering is Pablo Picasso's (1881–1973) *Guernica* (1937). (See illustration 4.4 for an image of *Guernica* at https://www.avemariapress.com/church-and-the-age-of-enlightenment-art.)

It represents the twentieth century as the world's most destructive, just as Leonardo da Vinci's (1452–1519) *Mona Lisa* (1503–1506) evokes the Italian Renaissance ideal of serenity and self-control. (See illustration 4.5 for an image of *Mona Lisa* at https://www.avemariapress.com/church-and-the-age-of-enlightenment-art.)

But *Consequences of War* and *Guernica* are not merely documents mirroring their times. They have the potential for personal and societal transformation, perhaps contributing something important to answering what can be done before an image of the seemingly overwhelming destructive force and human suffering.

The arts—painting, music, poetry, sculpture, theater, film, and fiction—are a distillation and intensification of life itself, revealing the archetypical or essences of reality. Those whose lives are quickened while hearing a piece of music, viewing a painting, or enjoying a play, as long as their dispositions and the conditions are right, experience, in attentive contemplation, something of the artist's experience of reality—that sphere of the unchanging, permanent things that matter greatly.

Who becomes an artist is often determined by the artist, by the society that he or she lives in, or by historians. Some artists make exquisite aesthetic objects that are not separated from everyday life, such as beautiful dishware, glassware, and furniture. Others strive to become part of an elite group of artists they consider to be exemplary, visionary, or famous. Artists may be formally educated, self-taught, or apprenticed in various ways. Even though a person may not be a maker of art—a great painter or musician, it is possible to become an artist or musician through virtuosic viewing and listening.

The archetype for all poets, the psalmist King David, expressed eloquently the transformative power of the arts, especially music. In Psalm 104, part of the Bible's wisdom literature, he committed himself to a life of singing and music to God, which he hoped would purify his thoughts, and thereby his interior life, so he would find joy:

> I will sing to the Lord all my life,
> make music to my God while I live.
> May my thoughts be pleasing to him.
> I find my joy in the Lord. (Ps 104:33–34)[10]

Chapter 5

The New Politics of the Enlightenment

Reasons of State: A Portrait of Cardinal Richelieu

The deep cold of winter did not in the least bother a mob from the extremist wing of the French Revolution determined to take revenge on history. It was 1793, a year into the revolution's Reign of Terror, and bloodlust had turned French politics into a war of all against all. The revolutionaries broke into the chapel of the Sorbonne, a college of the University of Paris founded by King St. Louis IX in 1253. Their target was enclosed in a smooth marble coffin, adorned with inscriptions and Baroque embellishment celebrating a man who had dedicated his life to the French state. The well-armed crowd surged toward the coffin and attacked the sculpted figure of the man lying within it with chisels, hammers, pikes, and rifle stocks.

Shrieking and howling, the mob pulled up a rotted corpse from the crypt. Urban legends circulated widely telling of Parisian waifs playing catch with its skull. All this rage against a man who lived and died more than 150 years before the Reign of Terror but who, nevertheless, symbolized the absolute rule of the French kings and the *ancien régime*—France's political and social order from the 1400s to the French Revolution of 1789. Cardinal Armand Jean du Plessis, whom we have known on these pages as Cardinal Richelieu, was essentially the prime minister of the French state under King Louis XIII from 1624 to 1642.

Richelieu has long been a lightning rod of controversy and cultish fascination. In *The Three Musketeers* (1844), Alexandre Dumas assigned him mysterious powers of detection and foreknowledge. His adversaries in the novel eat notes rather than burn them because they were sure Richelieu had the power to read ashes. Occultist fantasies aside, Richelieu was a brilliant intellect, master strategist, expert propagandist, and fanatical opponent of the Habsburgs and Spain. He read Greek and was fluent in Latin, Italian, and Spanish. His patronage of the arts was legendary, as was his personal library, which was among the best in Europe. He justified all of his decisions, even those of his own Church, as necessary for "reasons of state" (raison d'état). With the Treaty of Westphalia and the fracturing of a once united community of Europe, Richelieu's commitment to a strong, centralized nation-state, his sage-like statesmanship, and his skill of competing with great powers make him the father of modern nationalism and the new European order under which the Enlightenment thrived.

The Enlightenment: The Empire of Division

The previous chapter discussed ideas and their influence on the arts of learning, writing, painting, poetry, music, and culture in general. It considered the Enlightenment as a European and American renewal movement, one in a series of renewals or renaissances in Western civilization going back to the sixth century AD. Like earlier renewal movements, disruptive social and political events prompted the Enlightenment. The Enlightenment also shared in common with them a desire to make life a little better for everyone. But it differed significantly from them in its determination to sideline religion, and especially Christianity, from public life. Moreover, whereas previous renewal movements sought to unify society and synthesize Christianity with non-Christian cultures, the

Enlightenment moved decisively in the opposite direction. It was not a unifying force but a divisive one.

Emphatically, such division was not an accidental by-product of the Enlightenment project; it was intentional and baked into it from the start. Reason became separated from faith. Science and mathematics were severed from their historic relationship with the humanities. The human mind was recast as something akin to a calculating machine divorced from human emotion, will, experience, and the reality that minds exist in bodies, bodies that shaped the mind's view of the world and the way it reasoned.

The Enlightenment's preference for separation is nowhere more evident than in the relations between church and state and the organization of human communities. The enduring impact of the Enlightenment in our daily lives in the twenty-first century lies here in the Enlightenment view of politics, society, and human relations.

The negotiations and crafting of the Treaty of Westphalia at the dawn of the Enlightenment near perfectly exemplified the new European disunity and the dashed hopes for preserving a united Christendom. The Westphalia Conferences of 1644 to 1648 were the first all-European conferences since the Council of Constance in 1415. The latter dealt with affairs of the Church in the context of a united Christendom, whereas during Westphalia religion was incidental to its central focus: the affairs of individual states, war, and power.

The different interests of these two councils separated by just over two centuries was a measure of the progress of Europe's secularization. The hundreds of diplomats who participated in the Westphalia conference represented individual nations: Spain, France, Sweden, the Netherlands, Switzerland, Portugal, the various Italian city-states, and more than three hundred German states. None of them recognized or acknowledged any superior overarching loyalties beyond their nation-states, nor did they recognize their historical common ties. To the delight of nearly all European statesmen, all pretenses to European political or religious unity had been shattered. The new Europe was a large collection of disconnected sovereignties, free, isolated states acting according to their own interests. States exchanged ambassadors and created and dissolved alliances with other states in pursuit of their individual interest, changing their positions according to shifts in Europe's balance of power. After Westphalia diplomats and congresses of ambassadors crafted the public law of Europe. Westphalia was a new way for European nations to coexist. It served as the model for subsequent conferences, such as the Congress of Vienna of 1815, which settled the upheaval caused by Napoleon, and the Versailles Conference of 1919, which ended the First World War and redrew the map of Europe and its colonial interests.

Aside from a few regional conflicts in Ireland, Scotland, and Hungary, religion ceased to be an issue in European political affairs after 1648. The Treaty of Westphalia acknowledged the facts on the ground, namely, the reality of a Europe divided between Protestantism and Catholics. Pope Innocent X (reigned 1644–1655), who had declined to attend the Westphalia conferences, did not gently acquiesce to the new European realities, even though the Church was the one institution that could have prevented the fracturing of European civilization. He refused to sign any of the major and minor treaties that emerged from Westphalia and issued a formal edict or bull (a reference to the lean seal, *bulla*, that authenticated papal decrees) in November 1648 condemning and nullifying "in God's sight" the religion clauses in the Westphalian treaties.[1]

War fatigue permeated the Westphalia negotiations. The result was a patchwork of complicated compromises with no clear victor. To those who viewed the Thirty Years' War as primarily a war of religion differences, its inconclusive outcome undercut the notion that God had to be on one or the other side of the conflict. The impact of this stalemate on the mentality of Europeans cannot be overstated. The settled division of Europe between Protestants and Catholics required a new ethic of toleration and acquiescence to the reality of religious pluralism. Individual nation-states had to find ways to accommodate religious differences and maintain civil peace and order within their borders. One significant consequence of this new order was the sidelining of theology as the foundation of statecraft and public policy. In its place sovereigns looked increasingly to the new science of economics, hoping that greater material prosperity would distract their subjects from religious concerns.

Accompanying and strengthening this new reliance on economics were new conceptions of government and new bases for their legitimacy. The long-held principle that sovereigns held their office by divine sanction lost favor. A justification for the right to rule had to be found, and Enlightenment thinkers were at the ready to provide it. They looked past centuries of known, actual history and based their theories of government on an imaginative thought experiment: a hypothetical *state of nature*, where men and women had once existed before the advent of governments and civil society. It was an imagined birthplace of humanity in which there were no rulers, laws, schools, or any other institution of civic order. In this fictitious state, time stood still and human language was limited or nonexistent. Then, by some unspecified event, humans emerged from this state of nature to civil society, history began, and civilization developed.

The Enlighteners' state of nature was a deliberate appropriation of the biblical story of the Garden of Eden, where humanity transgressed a command of God and fell from grace. By their fall, Adam and Eve forfeited their prenatural, prehistorical infused knowledge (except for the knowledge of good and evil), the unity of thought and action, and bodily immortality.

The tale of Eden as a story of human origins and loss exerted great imaginative power in the development of Western civilization. It received a boost in the sixteenth century with the discovery of the Americas and the subsequent stories of its indigenous peoples that spread throughout Europe. As noted in an earlier chapter, the Enlightenment idealized the lives and social arrangements of the indigenous peoples of the Americas. The philosopher and political theorist John Locke, for example, celebrated the seemingly free-spirited, simple Native American ways of life as representing the original position of human beings before the organization of social and political life. "In the beginning," wrote Locke, "all the World was America, and more so than that is now."[2]

Locke, along with two other great Enlightenment philosophers, Thomas Hobbes (1588–1679) and Jean-Jacques Rousseau (1712–1778), assumed a hypothetical state of nature as foundational to their social and political doctrines. For all three, the accounts of America's original peoples lent a certain reality to these imagined beginnings. From these prehistorical beginnings, they proposed a radical program of social reform and engineering disguised as impartial speculations about human nature and the origins of human society.

Thomas Hobbes

Thomas Hobbes is the Enlightenment political thinker whose ideas most upended classical and Christian thinking about human nature, society, and government. Human beings in his conception of the state of nature were radically separated from each other—the epitome of the Enlightenment's empire of division. Violence and discord were everywhere and authentic human community nowhere. Life in the state of nature, he said famously, was "solitary, poor, nasty, brutish, and short." The state of nature was the "war of all against all."[3]

Considering the historical circumstances of his life, Hobbes's bleak picture of human existence is understandable. The state of nature mimicked life lived during the Thirty Years' War and the English Civil War. But circumstances played only one part in the development of Hobbes's political thought. More fundamentally, his view of human nature and the common life of humanity proceeded with impeccable logic from his materialist and mathematically rationalistic philosophy.

Let's first consider the world in which Hobbes lived most of his life and its effect on his writings. Hobbes was blessed with length of days— he died at ninety-one. He was a cautious man who detested violence of any kind, a disposition that took root at the tender age of four, when his father, a rather undistinguished clergyman in Westport, England, in a rage attacked another member of the clergy on the steps of his parish church. The embarrassment and subsequent scandal led Hobbes's father to flee Westport and abandon his family. The trauma of this desertion stayed with Hobbes for his entire life. Despite his family's precarious finances after his father left, Hobbes managed to acquire a superlative classical education, which provided him a solid foundation to engage energetically in the latest developments in mathematics and the experimental sciences.

Anticipating correctly the violence and terror of the English Civil War, Hobbes was among the first English intellectuals to emigrate from England to France in 1640. The English Civil War was a savage, divisive, costly, and murderous conflict that raged across England from 1642 to 1651, setting the forces of king against parliament and leading to the death of more than two hundred thousand English men and women. Hobbes escaped the worst of the violence in his homeland only to find himself in Paris in the midst of the French phase of the Thirty Years' War. Paris was mostly untouched by the violence of the war. Nevertheless it was the command center of the war, and the constant threat of a Spanish or Habsburg invasion hung over the city like a pall.

While in France, Hobbes became an active participant in the intellectual circle gathered around the great Catholic theologian, scientist, and mathematician Fr. Marin Mersenne. Fr. Mersenne was priest-friar in the austere Order of Minims, founded in Italy by St. Francis of Paola (1416–1507). The order expanded to France, Germany, and Spain. Like the Dominican and Franciscan, the Minims were mendicants who relied on the charity of others for their subsistence and the growth of their apostolic work. Mersenne was a prolific writer on a range of theological and mathematic topics, and renowned for publicizing and disseminating the work of some of the greatest thinkers of his age, including Blaise Pascal.

Fr. Mersenne steadfastly defended Catholic orthodoxy and held the traditional moderate view about human reason against two opposite positions prevalent in the Enlightenment. At the one end, there was the tendency toward overconfidence in reason's ability to know all there is to know about the material world and the means to control inanimate nature and social life. At the other end was a profound skepticism about reason's ability to know anything with certainty about the world. Hobbes was a champion of the former position; Pierre Bayle, whom we met in an earlier chapter, represented the latter position.

It is very likely that Fr. Mersenne's 1623 treatise *Frequent Questions Concerning Genesis* and its treatment of the human condition in the Garden of Eden sparked Hobbes's interest in the prehistorical state of humanity. For it was in Paris, when he was in close association with the Mersenne circle, that Hobbes brought to fruition his lifelong speculations about politics and the degree to which mathematics and the new experimental sciences could serve as the foundation for a new political and social order. The result of these speculations was *Leviathan*, completed in Paris and published in England in 1651. Emphatically, even though Fr. Mersenne had a great influence on Hobbes's mathematical and scientific reasoning, *Leviathan* was as far from Fr. Mersenne's thinking about politics as could be.

Leviathan is the book for which Hobbes is today most remembered and for which he was intensely vilified by his contemporaries. His name became a byword for atheism. His advocacy for a strong monarchy detached from any sort of spiritual guidance put him at the leading edge of Enlightenment reformers. Many Enlighteners and champions of the total authority of sovereigns celebrated Hobbes's argument for its promotion of an all-powerful central government, but they distanced themselves from his reputed atheism. For even though Christianity hung by a thread among seventeenth-century Enlightenment elites, most were not prepared to jettison Christianity entirely.

In Hobbes's state of nature there was no original harmony between God and humans, such as we find in Genesis before the disobedience of Adam and Eve introduced disorder into human existence. Rather, the state of nature for Hobbes was always a place of chaos and violence because humans left to themselves without any authority to keep them in line continuously squabble, fight, and instinctively resort to violence to settle any disputes. Hobbes speculated that people living in this fearsome and violent state of nature would at some point voluntarily agree to submit themselves to the rule of a strong man, a sovereign, who would suppress the inherent violence associated with base human nature and establish an ordered society. They would enter an irrevocable social contract by which they agreed to obey an all-powerful ruler, who would in turn protect them from physical violence and disorder.

Hobbes borrowed the image of leviathan, a creature from the biblical bestiary, to represent a body politic made up of all members of a post-state-of-nature society who had submitted themselves to a sovereign as their head. The sovereign merits his position because he protects each member of the body from the violence of other members. Emphatically, Hobbes's leviathan is a reference not to the sovereign alone but to all the members of society as a collective with the sovereign as its head. The great leviathan, wrote Hobbes, is "a commonwealth or state (in Latin, *civitas*)" whose purpose is for "protection and defense."[4]

Curiously, the biblical leviathan is the exact opposite of the Hobbesian leviathan. Hobbes's leviathan is a political society secure from unrest and disorder; the biblical leviathan refers to the serpentine Canaanite monster that from the beginning of time opposed the divine ordering of creation. Hobbes likened leviathan to "an artificial man," something not occurring in the natural world but more powerful and greater than nature. The sovereign of levitation is "an artificial soul" that gives "life and motion to the whole body."[5] Leviathan, as an artificial man, is brought into existence by human fiat (or will) that follows on from God's fiat recorded in the book of Genesis, "Let us make man" (Gn 1:26). So the sequence in Hobbesian logic is God makes man in a state of nature and then man makes the artificial man, called *leviathan*.

Hobbes also secularized St. Paul's conception of the Church as the Body of Christ with Christ as its head. "So all of us, in union with Christ," wrote St. Paul to the Romans, "form one body, and as parts if it we belong to each other" (Rom 12:4–5). To the Corinthians he wrote, "Just as a human body, though it is made up of many parts, is a single unit because of all these parts, though many, make one body. . . . If one part is hurt, all parts are hurt with it. If one part is given special honor, all parts enjoy it" (1 Cor 12:12, 26). Relying on the ancient Greek meaning of Church or *Ecclesia* as a public legislative assembly, Hobbes viewed the Church as merely one more political body among others. The notion that it was a spiritual, or mystical, body was literally "non-sense" in Hobbes's thinking because his strict materialist philosophy had no place for concepts like spirit.

Hobbes is a pivotal Enlightenment figure insofar as he provided a justification for secular rule totally independent from the spiritual guidance of the Church. *Leviathan* is a definitive, persuasive, and eloquent argument for why one ought to submit totally to secular governmental authority. Even if that government is imperfect, it commands obedience in order to prevent chaos, violence, and bloodshed. Subjects or citizens in the leviathan state can reject the authority of the sovereign in only the most extreme circumstances of malfeasance and abuse of power. The totalizing power of the monarch reflects Hobbes's own horror in hearing firsthand accounts of the beheading of England's King Charles I on the scaffold in front of the palace of Whitehall in 1649. The image haunted Hobbes incessantly. In part, *Leviathan* is a theory of government that would ensure that such a ghastly scene would never happen again.

To this end, Hobbes developed an elegant argument that interwove the idea of a social contract with the necessity of subjects' complete obedience and submission to sovereign authority. In Hobbes's view, men and women would eagerly assent to this social contract to escape the riotous pandemonium of the state of nature for the security of a society governed and policed by a powerful authority. People once having entered into this contract had a duty to keep obeying. The only right people might have to protest against their absolute ruler was if he or she directly threatened to kill them.

The suppression of opposition, the imposition of burdensome taxes, the disruption of the economy, and detainment of dissidents were not grounds for removing a sovereign. Hobbes conceded that a ruler might be tyrannical. Nevertheless, the people would still have a duty to obey him or her. For coercive power is a basic, unassailable fact of human community; without it the savagery of the state of nature looms threateningly. In Hobbes's words, "Though of so unlimited a power [of the ruler] men may fancy many evil consequences, yet the consequences of the want of it, which is perpetual war of every man against his neighbor, are much worse."[6]

Hobbes's theory was dark, cautious, and highly pessimistic about the common life of humanity. His antidote for this condition was philosophy, in particular the new Enlightenment philosophy. All Enlightenment *philosophes* turned to philosophy as a means for easing human suffering, reducing or eliminating conflict, and, in general, improving human well-being. But none more so than Hobbes. For him, philosophy was the means and ends of human community and government. The philosophy that underpinned Hobbes's *Leviathan* was a synthesis of three strands of Enlightenment thought: empiricism, the belief that what knowledge we have is acquired solely from our direct experience of the world; materialism, the belief that all we can know with our minds is matter and the behavior of material things; and determinism, the belief that there is no freedom in the world, that all things occur necessarily, determined by prior causes and independent of human or divine willing.

Hobbes quoted freely from the Bible, but the Bible had no serious influence on his thought. Hobbes rejected entirely any language about spiritual goods and the transcendent. Ideas such as soul or spirt, in his view, were metaphors for material objects. Feeling the spirit of another person meant for Hobbes an awareness of a memory of the other. The spirit of God that moved over the chaotic water in the book of Genesis referred to the wind, which could move water—no spirit, but a wind. Notions, such as soul, spirit, or any immaterial being, anything without a material body, anything that did not physically strike our five senses, are either metaphors for something physical or straight-out gibberish.

Because the only reality we know is material and bodily, then, for Hobbes, arithmetic and geometry, which are all about fixed and measurable relationships between things, are the subjects that tell us all we need to know about the world. Hobbes showed himself to be a loyal disciple of Isaac Newton in his devotion to mathematics as the sole pathway to certain knowledge of reality. But Hobbes went a step further than Newton in developing a theory of strict determinism that denied the existence of free will. In the realm of numbers and geometry, all relations are fixed and non-negotiable. For instance, there is no freedom when you calculate the third line of a triangle or the angle it forms with another line of the triangle. To demonstrate something arithmetically or geometrically is to demonstrate it with certainty because mathematical relationships are fixed. Hobbes thereby concluded that nature, which is wholly material, is governed by laws that are both mechanistic and wholly determined. There is no uncaused event, there is no chance, and there is no freedom in the world.

Hobbes stood out from his fellow Enlighteners for his bold and resolute application of his mechanistic view of inanimate nature to his conception of the human person, and social and political life. For Hobbes humans are physical organisms and behave no differently than other physical objects in the world. The brain is only matter governed by the same laws of nature that govern the inanimate world. Human beings, therefore, move and have their being in accord with the fixed laws of mechanics that govern everything else in the universe. From these assumptions, and without flinching, Hobbes drew the extraordinary conclusion that there is no such thing as human free will. What humans perceive as free will is the organism's instinct to avoid pain and seek pleasure. This simple pain-pleasure duality is the basis for Hobbes's entire theory of politics in *Leviathan*.

The human instinct to seek pleasure and avoid pain shapes human behavior. Without the threat of punishment for harming others, the drive of seeking pleasure and fleeing pain would compel each person to use all others as means to their own pleasure.

Such is the condition of men and women in the state of nature. Paradoxically, without the threat of punishment for harming others, the pleasure-pain principle drive would produce an unhappy state of affairs for humans. For the unchecked pursuit of personal pleasure leads inevitably to violence against others. The effect is a social free-for-all that makes life "nasty, poor, solitary, brutish and short," as Hobbes said—a life, in short, that is unlivable and fraught with anxiety and fear of others. Human well-being and flourishing then requires leviathan to alleviate an existence that would otherwise be unbearable. Hobbes granted a totalitarian power to sovereigns in order to keep order and prevent society from slipping back into the chaos that reigned in the state of nature.

By describing the state of nature in the darkest colors, Hobbes set exceedingly low expectations for what a good society should be. Anything better than the savagery of the state of nature was legitimate; rulers had no responsibility to do anything more than keep order and secure persons from physical violence.

Hobbes was the leading secular advocate for the unlimited sovereignty of the nation-state. It is the clearest, boldest statement of Enlightenment secularism. It takes as an unalterable given that violence is the permanent and fixed foundation of human existence and our common life. Force and violence are the first principles of human affairs. They cannot be changed but only be managed by counterforce, such as the threat of coercive punishment Beyond the management of violence, Hobbes denied there is any other higher good to which human society ought to aspire. For Hobbes, the peace established by politics is not, as it was in pre-Enlightenment Europe, a society that is ordered in such a way that persons can realize their best selves *in conspectu Domini,* in "the sight of God." Rather, the rigidly bounded coercive peace of *Leviathan,* for Hobbes, is merely the absence of war, which allows people to pursue their relentless quest for pleasure and avoidance of pain.

Up Close and Personal:
I NAPOLETANI: GIAMBATTISTA VICO (1668– 1744) AND ST. ALPHONSUS LIGUORI (1696–1787)

I Napoletani, the Neapolitans, Giambattista Vico (1668–1744) and St. Alphonsus Liguori (1696–1787), were highly regarded jurists, whose achievements ranged well beyond the practice of law. Both were extraordinarily well educated in the humanities, mathematics, and the natural sciences, and more than up to meeting the challenges that Enlightenment thought leaders posed to the tradition of Catholic thought and culture.

Although Vico and St. Alphonsus were a generation apart (Vico being the elder), they probably knew of each other at least by reputation because of their wide renown in the Naples law community. Both received their training in law from the University of Naples, and both were deeply formed by the storied history of Naples and its rich cultural, political, and intellectual life.

The ancient Greeks founded Naples around 600 BC as *Neapolis* ("New City") with great hopes that it would realize the high ideal of the city-state as the model of political community. It did so during the Roman Republic, when it became a major cultural center. In the medieval era, it became the capital of the Kingdom of Naples for centuries. The University of Naples, established by the Holy Roman Emperor Frederick II in 1224, is the world's oldest state-supported university, and the alma mater for one of its most famous students, St. Thomas Aquinas. Aquinas's *Treatise on Law* established the foundation of Vico's and Alphonsus's studies at the University of Naples. With the university as its center, Naples endured as a city of great learning in the arts and sciences, and particularly legal and political theory and practice.

Naples rose in prestige during the Enlightenment era, producing scholars and statesmen whose importance extended well beyond Naples. Chief among them were Vico and St. Alphonsus. To be sure, Vico is not a household name. Yet his breadth of knowledge, originality of thought, and influence on later artists and intellectuals, such as the Irish writer James Joyce and the English poet Samuel Taylor Coleridge, is palpable. His book *The New Science* was a groundbreaking critique of the secular Enlightenment project.

Born into a family of very modest means, Vico was surrounded by books from birth. His father, Antonio, ran a bookstore, which drew patrons as much for Antonio's jovial warmth as its impressive collection of books. When he was seven years old, Giambattista fell from a two-story building onto a stone-paved street and crushed the right side of his skull. The prognosis was death or a life of seriously impaired mental capacity. Happily, neither turned out to be true.

Following his recovery, Vico demonstrated intellectual talents far beyond his years. His first teachers were Jesuits, who recognized his abilities and challenged him to achieve ever greater heights of intellectual accomplishments. Often bored with institutional education, Vico repeated a cycle in which he would quit school and follow his own regiment of study in philosophy, mathematics, history, linguistics, aesthetics, and the law. After a while, he would return to school and then quit again. At age sixteen, he had advanced so far in the study of law that he was admitted to the bar. Those who watched him litigate predicted he would be a prodigy in Italian legal circles.

But Vico's passion was for the life of the mind, not the practice of law. One day while browsing in a bookstore, he met Monsignor Gerolamo Rocca, bishop of Ischia, a distinguished lawyer and fellow devotee of the philosophy of law. Vico's intellect so impressed Rocca that he hired Vico to tutor his two nephews. Vico jumped at the opportunity; it was a chance for quiet study with a salary.

Vico was a serious Catholic from boyhood. But his friendship with Monsignor Rocca deepened his appreciation of Catholicism and especially its great contribution to European civilization. Christianity, he wrote, made Europe "everywhere radiant with such humanity that it abounds in all the good things that make for the happiness of human life, ministering to the comforts of the body as well as to the pleasures of mind and spirit."[7] Such is not a bad characterization of the common good.

As a thinker, Vico grasped the importance of the questions raised by Enlightenment thought leaders. Yet for him, their answers to these questions were wrongheaded and misguided. He predicted with uncanniness the unsavory conclusions to which their calculating rationalism would lead. He rejected the Enlighteners' premise that the mind alone is what matters, and that it operates exclusively by rational categories. He argued that explaining and arranging social life by mathematical methods is to go "mad rationally." How can anyone attempt to travel by a straight line among the unpredictabilities of life, "as if whim, rashness, opportunity, and luck did not dominate the human condition."[8]

For Vico, truth was attained principally through not logical deductions patterned on the model of mathematical reasoning but reflection on the actions of men and women throughout history. His championing of history against Enlightenment rationalism put him squarely at odds with the culture of the Enlightenment. As we noted in an earlier chapter, the Enlightenment elites read history as a succession of criminalities, petty rivalries, and chicanery. History for them was no place to find truth and certainty. René Descartes, the focus of Vico's criticism of Enlightenment mathematized rationalism, relegated history to mere amusement for private interest, unsuited to serious attention. As one scholar of Vico's work put it, Vico's "Catholic piety alone" was sufficient to give him such a narrow dogmatic and limited view of the range and value of human knowledge for the common good.

Vico also engaged the secular state-of-nature Enlightenment thinkers. He criticized them for an overreliance on reason and its capacity to create a more perfect society. He especially objected to their overconfidence in the technology that went hand in hand with the overgrowth of rationalism. While immersed in the same issues as secular Enlightenment leaders, Vico was the first Western thinker to caution against the widely held optimism about continuous technological progress. Vico warned that an overreliance on technology as a solution to the problems of the human condition carried within itself the seeds of its own undoing and produced not human progress but human regress. People living in the twenty-first century, in the era of big tech, can judge for themselves whether Vico was right about an exaggerated faith in the power of technology to effect authentic human flourishing.

Our second Neapolitan, St. Alphonsus, is best known as the founder of the Congregation of the Most Holy Redeemer (the Redemptorists) and as bishop of Sant'Agata de' Goti. Like Vico, St. Alphonsus Liguori excelled at law and had an unconventional education before entering the University of Naples. He came from a prestigious noble family, long settled in Naples, and benefited from private tutors. His mother, Countess Anna Maria Caterina Cavalieri, oversaw his education and ensured that his religious formation was given pride of place in his upbringing.

At an early age, she placed him in the care of the Oratorians of St. Jerome, an order dedicated to the spiritual development of the sons of Naples' noble families.

St. Alphonsus's father, Count Giuseppe Liguori, was a naval officer and captain of the Royal Galleys. Giuseppe loved music and provided his son with a world-class musical education. With his father and music professor in attendance, Alphonsus practiced harpsichord and music theory three hours a day, and became a highly proficient performer and composer. When Alphonsus became a priest, he composed hymns and taught them to his parishioners. In 1732, he wrote his most famous hymn *Tu scendi dalle stelle* ("From Starry Skies Descending") as a pastorale—a musical form evoking the serenity of the countryside and memories of perhaps better, simpler days. St. Alphonsus based the hymn on his own original Neapolitan folk song, *Quanno nascette Ninno* ("When the Child Was Born"). In so doing, he sought to reanimate the fervor for holiness that his listeners might have had as children. (To watch Luciano Pavarotti's performance of St. Alphonsus Liguori's *Tu scendi dalle stelle*, see musical example 5.1 at https://www.avemariapress.com/church-and-the-age-of-enlightenment-art.)

Besides his outstanding musical talent, St. Alphonsus was a widely read poet and painter. But his main interest as a teenager was the law. Like Vico, he was admitted to the bar at the age of sixteen. Typical of his self-deprecating humor, he joked that he was so small of stature that his doctoral robes nearly buried him, which provoked laughter from those at court. Laughter notwithstanding, he quickly became the most sought-after lawyer in Naples, with a record of winning all his cases during his eight years of practice.

But like Vico, the practice of law was not sufficiently rewarding. Whereas Vico went on to an illustrious career as a professor at the University of Naples and influential philosopher, St. Alphonsus thirsted for a life devoted to God and holiness. In 1726 he took Holy Orders and began an apostolate to the urban poor of Naples and the surrounding countryside. Eventually, this work of catechesis and service led him to found the Redemptorist order in 1732.

St. Alphonsus's literary output was extraordinary: 111 works on spirituality and theology, translated into seventy-two languages. He remains the most widely read Catholic writer in the world. His greatest work, *Moral Theology*, is a nine-volume work written between 1748 and 1785 aimed at correcting the errors of a widespread heresy associated with Cornelius Jansen (1585–1638), a professor and rector of the Old Catholic University of Louvain in Belgium. Jansen and his followers exaggerated the effects of original sin on human nature and undervalued the redemptive power of Christ's mission. Like Calvinism, Catholic Jansenists held to a bleak and dark view of human nature, and subscribed to a severe doctrine of predestination, by which persons could do little if anything to effect their eternal salvation.

In *Moral Theology*, St. Alphonsus provided a balanced synthesis of divine law—written on the human heart, revealed by Jesus Christ, and interpreted authoritatively by the Church—and the importance of human freedom, a well-formed conscience, and the attractiveness and promise of a life lived in adherence to truth and goodness. Alphonsus advised priests to be charitable, understanding, and compassionate to those in their care, without relaxing the demands of Catholic moral teaching.

The severe doctrine of predestination and the stern moral precepts of Jansenism contributed to Enlightenment leaders' hostility toward the Catholic Church. Voltaire's brother was a strict Jansenist, which led him to despise and renounce Catholicism for what he mistakenly took to be its dour view of human nature and its tyrannical view of God. Other Enlightenment thinkers reacted to Jansenism by going to the opposite extreme. They denied original sin and insisted on exaggerating human goodness and perfectibility. According to Baron d'Holbach (1723–1789), Christians worshipped a "barbarous God." Nicolas de Condorcet (1743–1794), a leading Enlightener, claimed that "no bounds have been fixed to the improvement of the human faculties."[9] Moreover, the conflicts within Catholicism caused by Jansenism seriously damaged Catholic unity and hampered the Church's ability to focus on and provide a common front in answering the attacks of anti-Catholic Enlightenment intellectuals.

In the realm of politics, St. Alphonsus answered the new politics of the Enlightenment and its empire of division with recourse to the legal philosophy of St. Thomas Aquinas. Against the extreme individualism of state of nature theorists, such as Thomas Hobbes, Alphonsus reminded his readers that the law is not for the benefit of a single person but for the common good. Moreover, for St. Alphonsus, as for St. Thomas Aquinas, the source of vibrant political community and the enduring foundation of a good society is not the individual but the family.

In his general audience of March 11, 2011, Pope Benedict XVI recommended St. Alphonsus's apostolate as a model for the "new evangelization" of the twenty-first century, insofar as he prefigured Vatican II's "universal call to holiness." In the words of St. Alphonsus, all can attain holiness: "the religious as a religious; the secular as a secular; the priest as a priest; the married as married; the man of business as a man of business; the soldier as a soldier; and so of every other state of life."[10]

Pope Gregory XVI canonized St. Alphonsus in 1839, Pope Pius IX proclaimed him a Doctor of the Church in 1871, and Pope Pius XII named him the patron saint of confessors in 1950.

John Locke

John Locke is our second state-of-nature Enlightenment political philosopher. He was second only to his close friend Isaac Newton in the pantheon of Enlightenment philosophers. His two most influential writings, *A*

Letter concerning Toleration (1667) and *The Second Treatise of Government* (1689), established him as the father of modern liberalism. His influence on the American founding, which is the subject of the next chapter, was profound and everywhere present. Moreover, Locke provided post-Westphalia Europe with the philosophical justification for the new ethic of toleration. The Westphalia accords required a détente between Catholics and Protestants who resided in the same nation-state. Before Westphalia, toleration was unthinkable because, in effect, it gave stature to beliefs that differed from the prevailing religion of a particular state. Locke also provided the justification for the separation of church and state, which was another innovation necessitated by the division of Europe into discreet nation-states. We already saw that the Church was pushed to the fringes of the Westphalia negotiations. Developments in the seventeenth and eighteenth century continued this trend, such that religion became an entirely private affair with little or no effect in the public realm.

Locke was born into a sleepy village in Somerset, England, in 1632. He was ten years old when the English Civil War broke out. Locke's father served in the army of Parliament under the command of the Puritan leader, Oliver Cromwell (1599–1658). The public execution of King Charles I, the event that traumatized Hobbes just from hearing about it, occurred right before Locke's eyes, just a few feet away from his school. He never forgot the screams of the onlookers that echoed through the halls of Westminster Academy. After Westminster, Locke studied medicine at Oxford University but changed direction when he met Antony Ashley Cooper, the First Earl of Shaftesbury, who cut a dashing figure that captivated the young Locke. Locke joined Cooper's entourage in London, where under Cooper's patronage, he gained access to England's most prestigious scientific and philosophical circles, and gradually earned his way into the mainstream of European scientific thought and discovery.

Deeply troubled by the bloodletting in the religiopolitical English Civil War and the Thirty Years' War, Locke poured his intellectual energy into the question of religious differences. Religious conflict was no longer just a Catholic-Protestant issue, but a problem within Protestantism itself. The English Civil War raged between the English state church and the Puritans, who practiced a much more austere form of Christianity than the Church of England and the Roman Catholic Church.

Locke's argument for religious toleration proceeded as follows. A sovereign, government, or any human being is incapable of judging between the truths set forth among competing religious beliefs. Moreover, if they could, imposing one true religion would inevitably resort to the violent coercion of those who do not confess the one true religion. Such coercion toward religious uniformity would cause a greater amount of social disruption than allowing religious diversity.

The question of religious toleration led to Locke's thinking about the purpose of government, which, he said, was to preserve order in society such that men and women could live in social peace and material comfort. The state should have nothing at all to do with the good of their souls. Statecraft for Locke is emphatically not soulcraft. Thus, like Hobbes, Locke eliminated from government what had been its most essential tasks in pre-Enlightenment Europe: concern for God and the soul and, in general, establishing an ordered society that encouraged people to seek their material *and* spiritual well-being. For Hobbes and Locke the aim of government was merely to restrain and contain the base tendencies of human being that harm others, nothing more. The pre-Enlightenment concern of sovereigns for the common good of their states was jettisoned in favor of a regime in which each person sought whatever he or she found desirable. The new order proposed by Hobbes and Locke and realized gradually in America and in Europe created the conditions for an individualism that increasingly devalued the intrinsic value of a common life. The erosion of a robust sense of the common good typifies the Enlightenment tendency to separate and divide.

Locke's philosophy of toleration was the first step toward removing religion from the public square and privatizing it. Churches were reconceived as voluntary organizations that established their own rules of membership and doctrines. Locke's ethic of toleration was not immediately accepted by his contemporaries. But eventually it became accepted as a self-evident first principle such that any challenge to it became inadmissible, if not contemptible. Locke's achievement in this one book was truly remarkable. One man had set in motion a train of thinking that changed the entire Western world. Ideas do indeed have consequences.

Locke's next book was equally influential. Locke answered Hobbes's state of nature with his own version of it. *The Two Treatises of Government* begins with an imagined state of nature that predates organized political society. In contrast to Hobbes, Locke speculated that people in the state of nature were not people of violence and overly anxious for their bodily safety but rather reasonable and well-meaning individuals, who managed to get along with each other pretty well, even in the absence of public authority. People in Locke's state of nature had an innate sense of morality and human rights independent of government. They were the rights to life, liberty, and, above all, property.

Although life in Locke's state of nature was more congenial than in Hobbes's state of nature, persons in Locke's state of nature are not altogether able to win general respect for their individual natural rights. They cannot by their own efforts protect what is "proper" to them, namely, their property. Therefore, they agree to set up government and to surrender some degree of liberty to secure the rights of all. But they do so with no hint of Hobbesian fearfulness and panic. As in *Leviathan*, Locke's state-of-nature inhabitants enter into a social contract, but it is not unconditional, as it was for Hobbes, who gave all power and authority to a sovereign. Locke's social contract imposes mutual obligations. The people must be reasonable. True to the Enlightenment creed of reason, Locke insisted only rational beings could be politically free. Freedom is not an anarchy of undisciplined will;

it is the liberty to act without being compelled to do so by another. Only rational and responsible creatures can exercise true freedom.

For Locke, Hobbes's idea of acquiescing to life under a tyrannical rule for the sake of physical safety was unacceptable and perverse. Locke's social contract between rule and ruled was conditional upon the protection of individual property rights. If a government confiscated the personal property of those it governed, then the governed have a right to reconsider the social contract and, as a last resort, openly rebel against it. Locke agreed with Hobbes that rebellion is dangerous business, but it is less so than its alternative, which would result in a life of enslavement.

Although Locke's view of human nature and the common life was more sanguine than that of Hobbes, both set a very low bar for the aims of political society. In each case the government existed to provide order, for either personal safety and security or the protection of one's property. There was no sense of the common good, which was the aim of pre-Enlightenment, Christian, and classical political thought. Even if pre-Enlightenment regimes failed to live up to their Christian ideals, they never gave up on those ideals. Central to these ideals was the concept of the common good, the belief that human community is a fundamental good and not something one enters into out of fear and cautiousness. Both Hobbes and Locke had given up on creating a political and social order that drew people to the higher, more nobler ends of our common life.

Jean-Jacques Rousseau

Jean-Jacques Rousseau is our third state-of-nature, Enlightenment influencer. Rousseau was born to an educated watchmaker in Geneva in 1712. When he was ten his father got into a fiercely contested legal dispute, which forced the Rousseaus to flee Geneva. Jean-Jacques's life after Geneva was unsettled and often extremely lonely. He went to Paris when he was just coming of age. Its opulence, luxury, and affected manners contrasted sharply with Geneva, a city in the grip of Puritan severity and austerity.

In Paris he entered the salon circle of Madame Françoise-Louise de Warens (1699–1762), whom he met for the first time on Palm Sunday in 1728. She was Rousseau's tutor and benefactress, and eventually his lover. The two shared in common their Swiss, Protestant origins. De Warens converted to Catholicism in 1726 with a commission to spread Roman Catholicism near Geneva. Rousseau also became a Catholic under her influence. Her Catholicism notwithstanding, she was a controversial figure, who lived the sort of uninhibited life common to Parisian salon life.

Rousseau, for his part, was tireless in his pursuit of learning. He read constantly and was a keen observer of life. His personal successes and setbacks made his outlook on European society unique. At one point he waited tables; at another he was an attaché of the French embassy in Venice. He lived simply and frugally with his family in a Parisian side street and was an honored guest in the houses of European nobles. He was an accomplished musician and composer who resorted to copying music when his patrons abandoned him. He collaborated with Denis Diderot in publishing Diderot's famous *Encyclopédie*, a systematic dictionary of the sciences, arts, and crafts, published in France between 1751 and 1772. Rousseau wrote all of the articles on music for the *Encyclopédie*, which aimed to secularize learning away from the Jesuits. Rousseau lived his last years as an anonymous cottage dweller in a small French village. He was the only social critic of his time to have experienced European society from a variety of social positions.

Rousseau followed Hobbes and Locke in beginning his political theory with the state-of-nature hypothesis. In *The Social Contract* (1762), his most enduringly influential book, Rousseau echoed Hobbes in describing the state of nature as harsh and brutal without law or morality. Rousseau's state of nature did not borrow from the Garden of Eden; rather, his model was European society as it was before its regeneration by Enlightenment ideas and programs. For Rousseau, good people could be produced solely by an improved, enlightened society. Without this kind of improvement, he wrote, the human race would perish.

The social contract of Hobbes and Locke, by which people agreed to exit the state of nature and join civilization, was an agreement between a ruler and a people. Rousseau, by way of contrast, thought of it as an agreement among the people themselves. It was a social, not merely a political, contract. It was a contract that required each person to surrender his or her natural liberty to another, thereby fusing their individual wills into a combined "general will." In Hobbes's new order, the people made an irrevocable agreement to obey a sovereign. In Rousseau's, they agreed to accept the rulings of this nondescript general will as final. The general will was sovereign; as such it was absolute, sacred, and inviolable.

The concept of the general will is one of the most difficult to understand in the history of political philosophy. Rousseau's attempts at describing its nature are no help. It seems deliberately mystical, a kind of perverse version of St. Paul's version of the mystery of the Church as the Body of Christ. The general will was not determined by a majority vote. For Rousseau, the typical practices of democracy, such as debating and voting are inadequate to achieving or expressing the general will. For they would only create or exacerbate factional interests. He said little of the administration of government and did not have much use for parliamentary institutions. He was concerned with something deeper. A rather maladjusted outsider, he longed for a polity in which every person genuinely belonged and participated actively in its decisions and well-being.

Rousseau died in 1778 at the age of sixty-six. Whether he would approve or not, his writings were an enormous influence on the French Revolution, the subject of the next chapter. At the end of the day, the state-of-nature political philosophy, which provided the justification for the nation-state organization of Europe, co-opted the Judeo-Christian biblical and theological story of Eden and turned it into a supposedly real historical condition. The state of nature ought to have been a topic for theological reflection. It is instead a mistaken starting point for spooling out theories in an attempt to justify the legitimacy of nation-states and their governments.

YOU BE THE JUDGE:

Is the social contract the best way to view the human person and human relations?

The social contract is the notion that individuals' moral and political obligations depend on a contract or agreement among them to establish the political community in which they live. Thomas Hobbes, John Locke, and Jean-Jacques Rousseau, the main thinkers of this chapter, are the best-known advocates of the social contract. All three invite us to participate in a thought experiment: Imagine that at some point in the past all humans lived in a state of nature where there were no government or social institutions of any kind. Persons in this imaginary state of nature lived as equal and separate units.

In Hobbes's conception of the state of nature, each unit claims a natural right to what he or she likes irrespective of others. Locke, who was powerfully influential on American founding principles, places some limits on human freedom. Locke believed that in the state of nature, even with no governmental laws, humans respect each other's property rights, mostly for fear of a punishing retaliation for violating them. Rousseau's state of nature shares more in common with Hobbes's version than with Locke's because, like Hobbes, he sees individuals living in this state as totally free, unbound by any obligations to others.

All three states of nature assume a certain image of the human person—fully formed, independent individuals at the height of their cognitive powers, with the inner resources to shape their identities and the courses of their lives. Historians and philosophers have objected to this imaginary view of the unencumbered, atomized human person for ignoring the degree to which we are dependent on others in our infancy, childhood, and at other stages of life as well. As the philosopher Alasdair MacIntyre wrote, all of us exist on "a scale of dependence."[11] The development of the abilities necessary to grow and thrive in the world necessitates the near constant support of others—a web of unconditional, uncalculated care, concern, and gratuitous receiving.[12]

It requires the selfless and constant work of many others, known and unknown to us, to create a person's capacities for liberty and thriving, such as the discipline to defer gratification, to imagine and choose among alternative futures, and to gain knowledge about the world. Such fundamentals are never acknowledged by the social contract thinkers. Yet they are the ones required to become the independent rational individuals upon which they build their social and political systems. The popularity of their ideas have over time created the highly individualistic societies of Western Europe and America.

Intermezzo: The Arts as a Counterpoint to Societal Innovations

In the first chapter of this book we considered a painting of Peter Paul Rubens and a cantata by Heinrich Schütz as mirrors of society. Their works reflected the horrors of the Thirty Years' War. In this intermezzo we consider the arts as a counterpoint or countercurrent to the leading-edge movements of society. The state-of-nature political philosophers represented a strident secularism cloaked in biblical and religious language. As these new ideas gained acceptance among Western elites, the visual arts and music continued to express Christian ideals and values with confidence. Here are just two of many examples of the persistence of Christianity's influence in the arts: *The Virgin Appearing to St. Philip Neri* (1740) by the Venetian painter Giovanni Battista Tiepolo (1696–1770) and *Messiah* by George Frideric Handel (1685–1759). Besides their profound expression of the Christian faith, the link between the two works is the jovial St. Philip Neri, the apostle of Rome and the creator of the musical form we know as the *oratorio*.

Giovanni Battista Tiepolo

The last great painter of sacred visions, Tiepolo was all spirit and fire and the presiding genius of seventeenth-century Venetian painters. As a commercial and artistic hub of Europe, Venice thrived as a crossroad of trade, ideas, painting, architecture, and music. The discoveries of Isaac Newton were well known to Venetians, especially among their painters, whose influence dominated the European art scene. Tiepolo, for one, took full advantage of Isaac Newton's color wheel. Dark hues had characterized his earliest works. In the 1730s his paintings exploded with brilliance, such that he became known as the painter of light.

Ancient Greek and Roman philosophy and mythology dominated Tiepolo's early work. His most significant and deeply symbolic work, the massive fresco *Allegory of the Power of Eloquence* (1726), integrated classical pagan heroes, such as Orpheus, Amphion, Hercules, and Bellerophon, with Christian virtue and faith. The piece memorialized the Venetian Catholic aristocracy and did so by drawing heavily on the political philosophy of Giambattista Vico, whom we discussed earlier in this book.

As he matured, Tiepolo abandoned his early interest in secular subjects and turned to religious and mystical themes. This turn ran counter to Enlightenment secularization. At the same time he reappropriated the idea of light and redirected its focus onto the sacred. The starting point for nearly all of his religious painting was the Virgin Mary, protector of

Venice. In Tiepolo's *The Virgin Appearing to St. Philip Neri*, she is given pride of place. The painting was an altarpiece commissioned for a new Oratorian Church in the city of Cammerino.

St. Philip Neri was a humble man, famous for his sense of good humor, and extremely influential during the Catholic Reformation of the sixteenth century. He counseled Pope Pius V, Pope Gregory XIII, and Pope Sixtus V; served as spiritual director to St. Charles Borromeo; and was a close friend of St. Ignatius of Loyola. He founded the Priestly Society, known as the Oratorians, renowned for its get-togethers of people from all classes and religions to sing and pray. From these meetings evolved the musical form, known as the oratory—a sacred work based on biblical texts that combines vocal soloists, chorus, and orchestra.

In Tiepolo's altarpiece, St. Philip appears fully vested for Mass, with prominence given to the red maniple draped over his left forearm. Tiepolo would have known the symbolic meaning of the maniple. St. Alphonsus Liguori (1696–1787), a contemporary of Tiepolo and founder of the Congregation of the Most Holy Redeemed, explained that the priest used the maniple to wipe away the tears of the priest. In earlier times, "priests wept continually during the celebration of Mass."[13] These tears were mixed with joy, which captured perfectly St. Philip's constant joyfulness amid the trials suffered by the Church. As the priest lays the maniple over his forearm, he prays, "May I deserve, O Lord, to bear the maniple of weeping and sorrow, in order that I may joyfully receive the reward of my work."[14]

The reward is this vision of Holy Mother Mary with the child Jesus. St. Philip gazes upward in awe at the manifestation of the Mother of God and her child, surrounded by clouds and angels. Tiepolo's depiction of the material of Mary's robes is especially impressive, as is the mist-like feeling of the cloud, which renders the vision into an actual event.

For some viewers, this mistiness and St. Philip's upward gaze to the Madonna and Child evoke the uplifting spirit of music. Indeed, comparisons have been drawn between Tiepolo's combination of epic grandness and intimacy of detail with the music of George Frideric Handel, who managed the same effects in his oratorios. The strong link between Tiepolo and Handel lies in the figure of St. Philip Neri and the musical form of the oratorio. From its humble beginning in the rooms of St. Philip, the oratorio grew to its peak of popularity in Handel's London—the same city and at the same time that Hobbes and Locke were using biblical language to undermine the Christian foundations of European and American society. (For an image of Giovanni Battista Tiepolo's *The Virgin Appearing to St. Philip Neri*, see illustration 5.1 at https://www.avemariapress.com/ church-and-the-age-of-enlightenment-art.)

George Frideric Handel

The Thirty Years' War had been over for nearly forty years when Handel was born. But the terms of the Westphalia agreement significantly affected the government of Halle, the city of his birth. For one thing, his father lost his position as a court surgeon when the city's administration changed hands. Handel was baptized into the Lutheran Church, but the new environment of Halle fostered an influx of Calvinists and German Pietists.

Handel received an excellent education in classics, theology, and music. For a while he played violin for an opera orchestra in Halle, but he knew that to advance his compositional skills he needed to study in Italy. In 1706, he left Germany for northern Italy where he composed scared and secular music, and mingled with its leading composers. During an extended stay in Venice, he most probably encountered Tiepolo's paintings, which were the talk of the town. The intense Roman Catholic culture of Italy brought him to the brink of converting. But he never did.

In late 1710, Handel traveled to London for a premiere of his opera *Rinaldo*. London appealed greatly to Handel. With the ascension of George I (a German of the House of Hanover), Handel decided to settle permanently in London. In order to be active in public life, Handel had to enter the Church of England. Roman Catholics were violently suppressed in eighteenth-century England, but there were resistance movements to the Enlightenment in London that were gaining ground in Anglican circles. Unknowingly at the time, Handel's *Messiah* became central to this resistance.

Handel was the master of the oratorio form, and its serious treatment of biblical texts were a rebuke of Enlightenment secularity. Charles Jenner, who arranged the biblical texts for at least four of Handel's nineteen London oratorios, including, most famously, *Messiah*, took a poke at the Enlightenment cult of reason in the wordbook for *Messiah*. "Without Controversy," he wrote, "great is the Mystery of Godliness."[15] Jenner and nearly all of Handel's librettists (those who arranged the biblical readings for Handel's music) were High Church Anglicans averse to Deism—the Enlighteners' weak brand of Christianity. Handel and his librettists created a mainstream countermovement to the Enlightenment through the oratorio. They also were a means to heal the wounds opened up by the English Civil War. Oratorios provided a social space for Anglicans and Puritans to come together like no other cultural institution, helping to form a new national consciousness.

The narrative arc of *Messiah* is straightforward. Its first part prophesies the birth of the Christ; the second section, his sacrifice; and the third, the story of his Resurrection. *Messiah* could have easily been celebrated during Lent and Easter. But the popularity of Bach's *St. Matthew Passion* made little room for other music. So *Messiah* filled a void in Advent and Christmas music. By the early 1800s it became a staple of Yuletide in Britain and the United States. Mozart re-orchestrated *Messiah* in 1789, being careful not to tinker too much with the essence of Handel's music and orchestra. In Mozart's words, "Handel knows better than any of us what will make an effect. When he chooses, he strikes like a thunderbolt."[16] (For a performance of Handel's "For Unto Us a Child Is Born" from *Messiah*, see musical example 5.2 at https://www.avemariapress. com/church-and-the-age-of-enlightenment-art.)

Chapter 6

The Enlightenment in Action: The American and French Revolutions

Jesuit! A Portrait of Edmund Burke

Paranoia over a resurgent Roman Catholicism in eighteenth-century England ran high. Despite Handel's popularity and solid Protestant credentials, Handel's Italian operas, of which he wrote forty-four while in London, were under suspicion for their association with the Catholic city-states of Italy. Pamphlets critical of Italian opera fed worries that the Catholic states of Europe were plotting to depose King George I and enthrone the "Great Pretender," the exiled Catholic, James Francis Edward Stuart (1688–1766). "It is not safe," read one of these pamphlets, "to have Popish singers tolerated here, in England." Its author demanded a law that would require all "foreign singers, dancers, and tumblers to adjure the devil, the Pope, and the Pretender, before they appear in Public."[1]

English politicians drew even more scrutiny than performers if they had any trace of Roman Catholicism in their heritage. In the mid-eighteenth century, approximately 94 percent of Britons professed loyalty to the Church of England. Roman Catholics were a little more than 1 percent of Britain's population and were considered foreigners even though they were born and reared in Britain. The great bugbear of this anti-Catholic hysteria was the Society of Jesus, the Jesuits, who Britons believed were

139

intent on reclaiming Britain for Catholicism. The superior Jesuit educational institutions were also a threat to the Protestant establishment in England. English newspapers often discussed the Jesuit school at St. Omer's in Flanders, where many Catholic English boys were educated. It offered an education unmatched by any English institution.

So when the British press wanted to spread fear about the motives of the great statesman and philosopher Edmund Burke (1729–1797), it began with the false claim that he was an alumnus of St. Omer's. How else could a man born in Ireland rise to a seat in Parliament and dazzle its members and all of Europe with his keen intellect and eloquent oratory? Burke was Born in Dublin to a Catholic mother and Protestant father and was educated by Quakers and Anglicans. He was a committed member of the Church of England. Yet suspicions about his Catholic and Jesuit loyalties never abated. He was the ultimate scapegoat for any political or social failure that beset Britain. In the chambers of Parliament, it was not unusual for other ministers to call him "Jesuit" to his face. Newspaper caricatures of Burke in a Jesuit cassock were routine.

Burke was a pivotal figure in the Enlightenment. His writings on two of the practical political outcomes of the Enlightenment, the American Revolution of 1776 and the French Revolution of 1789, remain classics of oratory and political philosophy. Against the Enlightenment distrust and dismantling of tradition, Burke celebrated tradition as a teacher and a guide—a storehouse of human wisdom, which men and women ignore at great peril. The American Revolution, for Burke, exemplified a conservative revolution, in other words, a revolt to preserve the ancient rights of Englishmen against a king and parliament that abridged these rights. On the other hand, the French Revolution was an abomination insofar as it declared open warfare on the past and tradition, executing its king and setting up a tyrannical reign of terror that upended religion and centuries-old social and cultural practices.

Burke stood against the Enlighteners' preoccupation with mathematical reasoning as a tool to remake society and their disregard for what came before. He defended the common experience of men and women who meet the problems of social life by first consulting the mores and conventions of preceding generations. In sharp distinction from the Enlightenment leaders who held the past and tradition in contempt, Burke privileged them. They signified hard-won knowledge accumulated slowly over hundreds of generations. It was vanity for even the greatest men and women of genius to set their reason against the consensus of the ages. For Burke, inherited wisdom was far more reliable than the abstraction and theories of philosophes and denouncers.

In facing the challenges inherent in the human condition, Burke's first move was to consult what could be known from received traditions and common experience. How have humans met these challenges before? Were they successful? If not, why not? In privileging the wisdom of the past, Burke was not a hidebound, rigid traditionalist—far from it. Rather, he was known as the apostle of development, urging gradual reform and well-considered changes in social practices. Change is inevitable, he said, which if properly guided is an opportunity for renewal. A respect for the past, guided by reason—while aware of its limits—is a check against infatuation with the next new thing.

Burke was a constant critique of the state-of-nature political philosophers—Hobbes, Locke, and especially Rousseau. He dismissed the idea of a free, happy, lawless, and propertyless state of nature as sheer fantasy. Men and women were born into families and communities, not flung into existence as isolated individuals clawing out their survival in a relentless war of all against all. He thundered against the idolization of primitivism as somehow preferable to the life in advanced civilization. Human nature, he argued, was most itself when it was at its highest level of development, not in an unrefined state. Primitive simplicity is disastrous when applied to the matters of state and society. Burke wrote, "When I hear the simplicity of contrivance (meaning the fictional human and social origins in a state of nature) aimed at and boasted of in any new political constitutions, I am at no loss to decide that the [those who draft such constitutions] are grossly ignorant of their trade, or grossly ignorant of their duty."[2]

Against the regime of "naked reason"—his term for the Enlightenment political philosophers—he proposed a politics of prudence. Burkean prudence has nothing in common with current connotations of prudence, which convey guarded cautiousness. In the twenty-first century, the prudent person is often seen unflatteringly as the clever tactician who games out all possible outcomes to a course of action in order to take the least risky option or avoid personal commitment. This version of prudence contrasts sharply with the Christian prudence advocated by Burke. Prudence respects experience, one's own and the accumulated experience of generations. Closely connected with experience is memory, the recollection of real things and events as they really were and are.

Burke's politics of prudence, grounded in experience, tradition, and memory, was a rebuke to state-of-nature Enlighteners who began their political and social prescriptions not from reality but from an imagined beginning. In the midst of the Enlightenment's massive intellectual, social, and moral reorientation, Burke reminded Europe that prudence was and is the highest of human virtues, the mold and mother of justice, fortitude, and temperance—the other cardinal virtues. Taken together they enable all the powers of men and women for authentic human community in harmony with divine love.

An Empire of Reason

The American Revolution of 1776 is among the most significant events in world history. It absorbed the interest of European philosophes like few other events of its time. The leaders of the revolution, among them Benjamin Franklin (1706–1790), Thomas Paine (1737–1809), Thomas Jefferson

(1743–1826), John Jay (1745–1829), James Madison (1751–1836), and Alexander Hamilton (1755–1804), were themselves celebrated Enlightenment figures. Franklin was especially prominent and beloved by Europe's chic set. The personification of all that the Enlightenment held dear, he was a self-made man, insatiably curious about everything, conversant with the latest scientific literature, a shrewd politico and diplomat, and a Freemason. In 1751 he founded the Academy and College of Philadelphia, the forerunner of the University of Pennsylvania. In imitation of the Royal Society of London for Improving Natural Knowledge, Franklin organized the American Philosophical Society.

In December 1776, the Second Continental Congress of the United States dispatched Franklin to France to enlist French aid in the American war against Britain. It was a long game that Franklin played masterfully. Knowing the French enthusiasm for American primitivism, Franklin cultivated a simple, rustic persona that gave him ready access to the French court and the most fashionable salons. Beneath the quaint charm of the frontiersman—signaled by the coonskin hat he wore to French state dinners—was a sharp-eyed observer and practitioner of the courtly arts and rituals.

In February 1778, when the elderly Voltaire returned to Paris after an absence of nearly three decades, he and Franklin met in a flamboyantly staged interview. Before an audience of some twenty teary-eyed onlookers, Voltaire embraced Franklin and blessed Franklin's grandson in English, saying "God and liberty." The European and the American Enlightenments had met.

European Exploration and the Enlightenment: The Long Run-Up to the American Revolution

The story of the Enlightenment told in this book has made frequent reference to John Locke's famous declaration "In the beginning all the world was America." Locke spoke better than he knew. The European discovery of the Americas during the last decade of the fifteenth century opened up a global perspective for Europe that was foundational to the Enlightenment project. The new perspective pointed in two directions: backward to a romantic primitivism, exemplified in the state-of-nature political philosophizing that reordered European politics, and forward to the promise of a world order in which events anywhere on the planet resonate in unison within a universal, global society.

Christopher Columbus (1451–1506) arrived in the Americas in 1492, the same year that Lorenzo de' Medici passed into eternity. Although, the two were contemporaries, there is no record of them having met each other. Nevertheless, Columbus carried forward the Medici project of creative renewal with all the daring venturesomeness and energy that Lorenzo had set in motion in Florence. Columbus was not the first European to see the Americas, but he was the first to sustain the connection between the peoples of Eurasia, Africa, and the Americas, and thereby radically change the world.

Present-day anti-colonialist historians, college professors, and journalists tell a very dark, incomplete story of the encounter between Europeans and the indigenous peoples of the Americas. To be sure, profound cultural differences and missteps, misunderstandings, and, in the worst cases, naked greed led to abusive, exploitative, and inhuman behaviors toward the natives of the Americas on the part of European settlers. Europeans also unknowingly spread contagious diseases, such as smallpox, to the Amerindians. Europeans had built up immunities to these diseases, but indigenous Americans had not, and they died by the thousands as a result. Had another civilization, such as China, India, or Islam, made landfall in the Americas, which was a real possibility in the 1400s, similar contagions would have been equally devasting to the American natives.

Today's obsessive negative criticism of Europe's colonization of the Americas and other regions of the world has its origins in an

Enlightenment best seller, *History of the Two Indias*, published anonymously in 1770 in the Netherlands by Guillaume Thomas François Raynal (1713–1796). The book details how advances in navigation, ship design, and building and maritime trade created a "new kind of power" unknown before 1492. Raynal was French born, educated at the Jesuit school of Pézenas in southern France, and ordained a Catholic priest, serving in Paris for a while. The Church dismissed him for reasons unknown after which he became a writer and a journalist. For Raynal, European colonization ruthlessly exploited Indians, Africans, and Amerindians, turning commerce from a positive good to an instrument of deprivation and misery.

An exclusive focus on the adverse effects of Europe's expansion into the Americas obscures how Columbus changed the world for the good. In the words of one prominent historian, 1492 was "the year the world began"[3] because it marked the reunification of the human family. The history of the world before 1492 was one of divergence, difference, and separation. The divergence began about 175 million years ago with the breakup of Pangaea—the supercontinent that concentrated all of the Earth's land mass in one location. Continents and islands emerged and gradually drifted further and further apart. Each land mass developed its own unique plants, animals, and ecosystems. Humans, in turn, developed distinctive cultures based on their physical locations. The diversity of human cultures had widened to the degree that when contact between them occurred, such as in 1492, they often failed to recognize each other as human. Some Europeans wondered whether Amerindians were human; some Amerindians thought Europeans were demigods.

The Euro-American contact of 1492 reversed this history of divergence with extraordinary speed. Humans that had been scattered and isolated around the globe regrouped. Columbus's mission reconnected the world, so that today the entire world is webbed together. Our experience of a closely knit world is a little more than half a millennium old, a period of time dwarfed by the millions of years of physical divergence. Columbus's achievement was a monumental scientific achievement driven by a Christian sense of energy and mission. Before Columbus's voyage, the oceanic winds were an undecipherable code. The European navigators of the fifteenth century assembled by Prince Henry the Navigator cracked the code, and Columbus used it to cross the Atlantic and return to Europe.

It was Servant of God Bartolomé de las Casas (1484–1566), Columbus's de facto literary executor, who saw the unification of humanity as the great significance of the Columbian project. Living among the Taino, the Amerindians who first met Columbus on the islands of what are now known as Haiti and the Dominican Republic, he was steadfast in proclaiming the common rights and solidarity of all peoples of the earth. What was difficult for others blinded by the experience of human divergence to see, de las Casas saw with perfect clarity and certainty: that, indeed, all men and women belong to the human family, created by God to participate in building the kingdom of God on earth, which will one day find its fulfillment at the end of time when the earthly city and the heavenly city of Jerusalem are made one and the same.

De las Casas and his Dominican confreres were the first to protest the mistreatment of indigenous Americans, a protest that eventually led to King Ferdinand of Spain and Pope Pius III to insist on the humanity shared in common between American natives and Europeans. On the First Sunday of Advent, 1511, Dominican Fr. Antonio Montesino preached a landmark sermon to the Spanish nobility living in the Americas. In the style of St. John the Baptist—a voice crying in the wilderness—he upbraided the Spanish: "You are now living and dying in a state of mortal sin, on account of your cruelty and tyranny over these innocent people. . . . Are you not bound to love them as yourselves? Have you lost your reason, have you lost your senses or are you buried in a lethargic sleep?"[4]

King Ferdinand, upon hearing of the subhuman treatment of the Amerindians, commanded that they be treated with the same dignity and rights as Europeans and all other peoples. Pope Paul III (reigned

1534–1549) saw the history of divergence that led Europeans to see American natives as other than part of the human family as diabolical. In his famous bull *Sublimis Deus* (1537), known as the Magna Carta for human rights and the basis for the Church's ethic of solidarity, Paul III wrote:

> The [native Americans] and all other people who may later be discovered by Christians, are by no means to be deprived of their liberty or the possession of their property, even though they be outside the faith of Jesus Christ; and that they may and should, freely and legitimately, enjoy their liberty and the possession of their property; nor should they be in any way enslaved. . . . [The American natives] and other peoples should be converted to the faith of Jesus Christ by preaching the word of God and by the example of good and holy living.

The Christian evangelization of the Americas also shifted the balance of world religions. Before 1492 Islam's territorial reach extended far beyond that of Christendom. Afterward, Christian civilization exceeded Islamic civilization in the number of adherents and in territory.

Until Columbus's Atlantic crossing Europe was a backwater on the Western edge of Eurasia, inferior in most aspects to China, India, and the nations of Islam. Between 1492 and 1600, Spain had settled nearly all of coastal South America (except Brazil), Central America, the Caribbean, and large sections of North America. The Spanish settlement was unprecedented in human history. In two generations Spain acquired more territory than Rome conquered in five hundred years. Genghis Khan (1162–1227) ranged over a greater area (in Asia) but left only destruction and devastation behind, whereas for good and for ill the Spanish organized and administered all the lands and peoples under their rule.

The Americas and Europe's Great Powers Rivalries

The other great powers of Europe followed Spain into the Americas. The Dutch, persistent rivals of the Spanish, established trading posts and settlements along the Essequibo River in the northern area of South America during in the 1590s. Later, following exploration and the establishment of trading expeditions in North America, the Dutch settled their first colony in North America in 1615 at Fort Nassau, on Castle Island along the Hudson River, near present-day Albany. Although the official Dutch presence in North America gave way to the English in the later part of the seventeenth century, the Dutch had created the key financial and quasi-political institution by which Europe expanded into the Americas, Asia, and Africa: the Dutch East India Company or VOC (Verenigde Oost-Indische Compagnie).

Founded in 1602, the Dutch East India Company was preeminently an Enlightenment institution. It was a company-state, unique among the emerging nation-states of Europe. The VOC was a large, multinational business corporation with the characteristics of a sovereign nation-state, having its own army, navy, currency, legal code, and diplomatic corps. Its leaders blended a tolerant strain of Dutch Calvinism and a commitment to moderate Enlightenment ideas. Through their significant commercial and political influence, they sought to extend Enlightenment ideas to Asia, Africa, and the Americas. The VOC was a direct forerunner of the twentieth- and twenty-first-century global business corporation, which cuts across the international system of state sovereignties, dominating the world's economic systems and disseminating progressive Enlightenment doctrines. Other European nations imitated the VOC model, but none managed to combine the commercial and state functions as thoroughly as the VOC did. It was and continued to be an underappreciated socio-politico-economic force in spreading Enlightenment ideas beyond Europe.

In 1607, eight years before the Dutch settled Long Island and the Hudson River Valley, the English established Jamestown in 1607 in what is now Virginia. A year later Samuel de Champlain led a group of French colonists down the St. Lawrence River to found Quebec in 1608. Before her abdication, Queen Christina of Sweden sponsored an expedition to

North America in 1638. The result was New Sweden, centered in the Delaware Valley, extending to sections of present-day Delaware, New Jersey, and Pennsylvania. The Swedes eventually surrendered their colony to the Dutch in 1655.

While the Thirty Years' War consumed the attention of Europe's continental powers, the English secured their hold on the Eastern Seaboard of North America. The English settlers in these colonies were overwhelmingly Protestant, representing Puritans, Anglicans, Quakers, and Baptists, among others. England's internal political struggles and a succession of wars with France and its allies distracted its attention away from the American colonies from the 1630s to 1763. During these years, when it came to the Americas, the English government defaulted to a policy of benign neglect. England decisively defeated France in 1763 in the French and Indian War (the Seven Years' War as it was known in Europe). But the cost of doing so was exorbitant. The debt accumulated by the British crown nearly bankrupted the nation. Desperate for cash, England sought new revenue streams. King and Parliament could not squeeze anything more from their own subjects living in the British Isles. Englishmen were already the most heavily taxed people in Europe in the mid-1700s. So England turned to the American colonies for money, departing from its policy of benign neglect. Reasoning that America should pay their fair share for the protection provided them by the British army and navy, King George III (reigned 1760–1820) through his ministers began levying taxes on the American colonies.

The colonists did not object to these new taxes for their financial cost, which was minimal, but on principle. The Stamp Act of 1765 was a complete shock to the Americans. It was the first direct tax on the colonies by the British government. The act required that all legal documents be drawn up on specially stamped paper, showing proof of payment. The legality of contracts of any kind—property deeds, wills, and marriage licenses—was invalid in a court of law unless they were drafted on paper bearing the British stamp. Additionally, newspapers, playing cards, and dice had to bear the stamp.

It is not that American colonists were untaxed. Rather, they had developed their own legislative policies and practices for levying taxes. In their haste to acquire new revenues, the British ignored this 150-year-old colonial American system for levying taxes.

The actions of king and Parliament seemed reasonable from their perspective. Americans benefited from English protection against the French and the indigenous American tribes. The new taxes were aimed at having the colonies pay their fair share of the cost of their own defense, which accounted for less than one-third of the cost of maintaining British troops in the colonies. But Americans saw no need for a British military presence in their colonies. The French had been defeated, and the Americans proved they could defend themselves in the French and Indian War. Under the new British impositions, the Americans were sure the British garrisons in the American colonies were now there to surveil them and curtail the political, religious, and economic freedoms they had come to enjoy.

Americans bristled under the new regime of British taxation and the growing military presence to enforce it. But few colonists wanted or even imagined independence from Great Britain. In 1775, less than one-third of Americans favored independence. For example, in the late 1760s John Dickinson of Philadelphia (1732–1808), who in 1776 refused to sign the American Declaration of Independence from Great Britain, raised the possibility of independence, but only to register the shock and horror of such a move.

In the year following the French and Indian War, Americans were proud to be British subjects. They were part of the largest, most powerful empire in the world.

Their argument with King George III and the British Parliament was a conservative one based on tradition: the British had violated Americans' ancient rights as Englishmen. The essence of their case was that they were

British subjects, and thereby entitled to the same privileges as their fellow subjects in the mother country. To be sure, those living in England paid higher taxes, but Americans paid much more in blood, sweat, and anguish. All the land that was cleared in the Americas; the wars with native tribes and the French; and the brothers, fathers, and sons who perished in building the colonies that enriched the British Empire made the stamp tax and subsequent taxes insulting and abusive.

In 1763 James Otis Jr. (1725–1783), a member of the Massachusetts provincial assembly, put the colonials' position succinctly:

> That the colonists, black and white, born here are freeborn British subjects, and entitled to all the essential civil rights of such is a truth not only manifest from the provincial charters, from the principles of the common law, and acts of Parliament, but from the British constitution, which was re-established at the Revolution with a professed design to secure the liberties of all the subjects to all generations.[5]

Tensions between the British government and the Americans quickly intensified. In reaction to the 1773 Boston Tea Party, in which colonists dressed as native tribesmen dumped boxes of tea into Boston Harbor, King George III ordered the closing of Boston Harbor. Parliament followed quickly upon the king's action with a move against the Massachusetts colony, declaring it in full, open rebellion against the crown. In April 1775 General Thomas Gage, commander in chief of British forces in North America, launched an offensive to seize the colonials' arms and other war materiel. American militiamen engaged the British at Lexington and Concord, Massachusetts. The ferocity of the fighting shocked both sides and significantly escalated the British-American conflict.

The Battles of Lexington and Concord brought about what had been until 1775 an elusive quest for unity among the thirteen colonies. The colonies remained highly protective of their individual interests, but they recognized that what happened in Massachusetts could happen to any one of them. So they came together in a series of conferences, culminating in the Second Continental Congress convened in Philadelphia in May 1775. Its purpose was to govern a loose confederation of thirteen colonies. Congressional members met, ignoring warrants issued by the British army for treason. They established a continental army, printed currency, and established committees to deal with domestic and foreign affairs. Still, few members sought independence from Great Britain.

By late spring 1776, American colonists had lost most of their civil liberties under British military occupation, and their negotiations with King George III were getting nowhere. Spurred on by the publication of Thomas Paine's Radical Enlightenment pamphlet, *Common Sense*, in early 1776, the colonists moved decisively toward what was previously unthinkable: independence. Before doing so, they felt compelled to explain themselves to the world. It would not be just a list of grievances directed to the king and Parliament. They had already gone that route with no benefit. With an Enlightenment confidence in the power of reason, the Congress struck a committee of five to draft a declaration justifying independence. Benjamin Franklin, John Adams, and Thomas Jefferson were among the five, with Jefferson writing the first draft. Jefferson knew this document had to be persuasive to many audiences. Ordinary Americans would read it and be convinced to support independence. Fair-minded Englishmen would read it and urge restraint upon the king and Parliament. European governments would read it and provide military and financial assistance to the new continental army.

Like Franklin, Jefferson embodied the ideals and the culture of the Enlightenment. He was well educated, well-traveled, fluent in French and Italian, and a more than decent violinist. He kept current on the new scientific knowledge, keenly observed the natural world, dismissed creedal religions, tinkered obsessively in the fashion of Benjamin Franklin, and founded the University of Virginia as the secular foil to his Anglican alma mater, the College of William and Mary.

Jefferson's declaration was a near-perfect realization of Enlightenment principles. It was a manifesto championing universal rights based on the clear evidence of reason that would inspire liberation movements for more than two centuries. To be sure, there were many influences on the American Revolution—religious, economic, and a 150-year tradition of self-government. Nevertheless, the Enlightenment influence on the minds of the American founding generation was primary and proved to be the most enduring. Of particular importance was John Locke's theory of government as a contract between rulers and ruled. According to this contract, a people could cast aside inherited political institutions with abandon if they did not serve the interests of the current generation.

Thomas Paine's influence was not as enduring as Locke's, but his pamphlet, *Common Sense*, fed Americans' rage against Britain's abuse of its authority. Written in the form of a sermon, Paine linked independence with the common tradition of dissenting Protestant beliefs as a way to construct a distinctly American political identity.

The declaration's preamble universalizes the American colonists' dispute with the crown and the Parliament, which in previous centuries would be viewed as a localized, internal dispute among subjects or citizens of one nation. As John Adams said upon reading the first draft, it was something altogether unexpected, a statement not only of American independence but also of the rights of all peoples. The preamble resists any mention of the American complaint with the British. Rather, it takes an abstract tone, imitating the way an Enlightenment philosopher or scientist would approach a subject. It has an air of objective detachment from the partisan issues involved in the dispute between the motherland and its colonies. The declaration adopts the style of a scientist describing the causes of any physical event.

The declaration opens with an eloquent, magisterial oratory, casting the movement for American independence as an inevitability within the grand sweep of history. In soaring words, Jefferson wrote:

> When in the Course of human events, it becomes necessary
> for one people to dissolve the political bands which have con-
> nected them with another, and to assume among the powers
> of the earth, the separate and equal station to which the Laws
> of Nature and of Nature's God entitle them, a decent respect to
> the opinions of mankind requires that they should declare the
> causes which impel them to the separation.[6]

Jefferson presented the American separation from England as "necessary," sanctioned by "the Laws of Nature and of Nature's God." In the
eighteenth century the word *necessary* suggested something inevitable,
the product of a fixed natural law that was outside the control of human
beings. Cast in this light, the American revolt against England was not
the result of decisions made by people but an action that was inescapable
and unavoidable, similar to the movement of the planets, the ebb and flow
of tides, and the change of the seasons in the physical world. The issues
set out in this preamble are characterized as a contest of principle, which
when laid bare before "the opinions of mankind" legitimize the rightful-
ness of America's decision for independence—all of this without a single
mention of Britain or the American colonies.

Although the various Protestant denominations were everywhere
evident in revolutionary America, the preference for Enlightenment principles became clear in the revisions to Jefferson's first draft of the declaration. The final draft reads, "We hold these truths to be self-evident, that
all men are created equal, that they are endowed by their Creator with
certain unalienable Rights, that among these are Life, Liberty and the
pursuit of Happiness." Jefferson's first draft read, "We hold these truths
to be sacred and undeniable."[7] Even though the meaning of "sacred" had

been hollowed out in Jefferson's use of it, its overtone to Franklin's ears were still out of place in the document. He replaced "sacred" with "self-evident," a favorite term of Enlightenment philosophers.

The declaration's stirring words aimed at convincing Americans to put their lives on the line for the cause of independence. For most colonists, separation from the mother country threatened their sense of security, economic stability, and identity. The preamble sought to inspire and unite them through the vision of a better life. Printers worked day and night to produce copies of the declaration, which was read aloud in town squares, churches, and pubs. Although the decision for independence was by no means unanimous, these Enlightenment ideas and writings radicalized enough Americans that they took up arms against the mightiest empire on the globe.

The colonists fought a war for liberation they could not win on their own. The persuasive power of the declaration was not enough to draw Britain's competing great powers of Europe into the war on the side of the Americans. It took an American victory over British forces at the Battle of Saratoga in 1777 and Benjamin Franklin's skilled diplomacy to convince France to join the war on the American side. The French commitment emboldened Britain's historic enemies, the Dutch and the Spanish, such that what started as a civil war between Britain and its colonies expanded to a global world war between the European great powers. Britain could no longer focus only on a land war in the Americas. It now faced the threat of an invasion from a second armada led by Spain and France, and naval engagements in the Caribbean and India with the French, Dutch, and Spanish navies.

In October 1781, the ground war for American independence ended when French and American forces surrounded the British position at Yorktown, Virginia. Two years later, the British and Americans signed the Treaty of Paris, which gave America its independence.

With historians' tight focus on the British-American colonial revolt, it is easy to miss the actual North American geopolitical realities at the end of the British-American War for Independence. The British-American colonies, which after 1776 became states, occupied a fraction of North America's land mass. They huddled against the Atlantic coastline, dominated by various Protestant sects, but surrounded on the west and south by an overwhelming Catholic presence. Most of what would eventually become the continental United States of America in 1776 remained inhabited by numerous Amerindian tribes, the French, and the Spanish.

While the War for American Independence raged in the eastern part of the continent during the 1770s and early 1780s, St. Junípero Serra (1713–1784) established a chain of nine missions along the California coast, which eventually grew into major American cities. Among the most significant of these were the Mission Basilica San Diego de Alcalá (founded on July 16, 1769), which is present-day San Diego, and the Mission San Francisco de Asís (founded on June 29, 1776), present-day San Francisco. St. Junípero would have founded a mission north of the Mission San Francisco had he not met Russian colonists and Russian Orthodox missionaries who had settled Alaska and moved from there south along the coast of California.

In 2015, Pope Francis referred to St. Junípero Serra as "one of the founding fathers of the United States."[8] He was, however, guided by principles other than those of the British-American founders. Besides the Gospel and the example of St. Francis of Assisi, Serra's intellectual influences were St. Bonaventure and Blessed John Duns Scotus. He brought to the American West a broader legal and historical tradition that, in principle, was as much concerned with freedom and human rights as the enlightened Founding Fathers on the East Coast.

The French Revolution

Social, economic, and political turmoil followed in the immediate aftermath of America's War for Independence, both in the newly founded United States and in France, its principal ally. By the end of the 1780s, the US Constitution established a new political order based on English history, the ancient Roman republic, and the ideas of major enlightenment treatises, such as John Locke's *Second Treatise of Government* and Baron de Montesquieu's *The Spirit of the Laws* (1748). The situation in France was quite different. In July 1789 France erupted in a revolution that destabilized France and all of Europe for the next quarter century.

The causes of the French Revolution are many. Socially, its roots lie in a long-standing rigid class system that benefited a privileged aristocratic and clerical elite at the expense of the middle class and the urban and rural poor. In the realm of ideas and beliefs, there was the wide circulation of new anti-tradition and anti-Catholic Enlightenment ideas. Economically, there was the enormous debt incurred by Louis XVI (reigned 1774–1792), in large part to pay for the war in the Americas. Like the American revolution, taxation was the immediate concern overlaying much deeper issues of principle and pent-up frustration with the regime of Louis XVI, which spent lavishly on its court but provided little assistance to a population suffering from twenty years of poor harvests, drought, livestock diseases, and exorbitant bread prices. Rioting, looting, and strikes were commonplace during the reign of Louis XVI.

In 1786, Louis XVI's chief financial minister, Charles Alexandre de Calonne, proposed a financial plan that included a universal land tax from which the privileged classes—the nobility and religious—would no longer be exempt. De Calonne's proposal undid centuries of French policy and would obviously meet serious opposition from the aristocracy and the Church. To counter this opposition, Louis XVI convened the Estates-General, an assembly of religious, nobles, and middle-class artisans and merchants that had not met since before the Thirty Years' War.

Each of the three estates caucused individually to draw up a list of grievances to present to the king in preparation for a combined meeting of all three estates on May 5, 1789. The clergy gathered as the First Estate, the nobility as the Second, and all other classes as the Third.

The Third Estate represented the largest number of Frenchmen—over 98 percent of the population. But it could be outvoted by the other two estates. In the run-up to the May 5 meeting, members of the Third Estate organized a campaign in support of equal representation and the termination of the noble and clerical vetoes. The highly public debate on proposed voting reforms escalated into outright hostility between and among the three estates, overshadowing the original purpose for the convention of states and the authority of Louis XVI. Unable to reach an agreement on voting prerogatives, the First and Third Estate combined and declared their union to be the official representative assembly of France under the name of the National Assembly. The French clergy thereby voluntarily gave up its centuries-old exemption from taxation. Shortly thereafter, forty-seven members of the Second Estate joined the new National Assembly.

On June 12, less than six weeks after Americans celebrated the inauguration of George Washington as their first president, the French National Assembly met at Versailles to draft a new constitution in imitation of what the Americans had done in Philadelphia during the summer of 1787. Whereas the delegates to the Philadelphia conference worked in an atmosphere of comparative civil peace, fear and violence enveloped the delegates to the Versailles conference. Panicked by a potential royal backlash to the recent events, on July 14, 1789, Parisians rioted and stormed the Bastille prison and fortress, the symbol of royal absolutism. The French Revolution had begun.

What started out as a dispute over voting rights escalated quickly into waves of violence and hysteria. As unrest spread from the cities to the countryside, the long-exploited peasantry looted and torched the homes of tax collectors, landlords, and the remnants of the feudal manorial lords. Fearing for their lives, the agrarian nobility abandoned their estates for the safe haven of the cities. The rural uprising prompted the new National Assembly to abolish feudalism on August 4, 1789, signaling the end of the prerevolutionary political order: the ancien régime.

The New Order and the Declaration of the Rights of Man

Like their American counterparts, the French revolutionaries felt compelled to declare their aims to the world. In August 1789, the National Assembly commissioned and ratified the Declaration of the Rights of Man and of the Citizen, a statement of democratic principles.[9] Unlike the American Declaration of Independence's dependence on John Locke political ideas, the French declaration drew heavily on another social contract theorist, Jean-Jacques Rousseau. The French declaration announced the National Assembly's agenda of replacing the ancient régime with a new order committed to equal opportunity, freedom of speech, expansion of voting rights, and self-government.

Embodying these commitments in a written constitution for a new government, such as the Americans had done in their constitution of 1781, was a greater challenge for the National Constituent Assembly than it was for the ad hoc committee that drafted the Philadelphia constitution. Both groups faced similar questions, such as the selection of representatives to the new National Assembly, the relation of Church and state in the new regime, and the relation of the assembly to the executive or the king. In the French case the monarchy was the trickiest to fit into the political system.

The final draft of the French constitution adopted on September 3, 1791, reflected the influence of the National Assembly's moderate elements. Much like the British system, the French constitution established a constitutional monarchy that gave veto power to the king and the authority to appoint government ministers.[10] However, the extremist wing of the

French Revolution opposed the remnants of monarchy in the constitution. Maximilien de Robespierre, Camille Desmoulins, and Georges Dan-
ton campaigned for a republican form of government along the lines of
the ancient Roman republic and the new American republic. They also
insisted on putting Louis XVI on trial.

With the ratification of France's new constitution, the National Assembly disbanded, replaced by the newly elected Legislative Assembly. Among
the first acts of the new assembly was a declaration of war against Austria
and Prussia—states harboring French émigrés who were assembling a coalition of counterrevolutionaries to retake France and restore monarchal
rule. The war also had a missionary aim: to spread Enlightenment ideals
and revolution across Europe by conquest.

Meanwhile, on the home front, the French Jacobins, the most extremist elements of the revolution, invaded the royal apartments on August
10, 1792, and arrested the king and his wife, Marie Antoinette. Six hundred Swiss guards made a heroic but unsuccessful defense of the royal
family. The capture of the king set off waves of violence in which Parisian
insurrectionists massacred hundreds of counterrevolutionaries, bishops,
priests, and women religious. The Legislative Assembly was replaced by a
National Convention, which declared the total abolition of the monarchy
and the establishment of the French republic. On January 21, 1793, the
National Convention ordered the execution of King Louis XVI for high
treason and crimes against the state.

The Reign of Terror

In June 1793, the Jacobins seized control of the National Convention from
the moderates and began a series of measures designed to erase the French
past and particularly its Catholic influences. The convention replaced the
Gregorian calendar with a "calendar of reason" bearing new names for the
months and a ten-day week, in order to abolish the Sabbath. September 22
became New Year's Day to memorialize the overthrow of the monarchy on

that date in 1792. Officers of the convention turned churches into "temples of reason," to commemorate the victory of the Radical Enlightenment. They crowned a prostitute as the "Goddess of Reason" in Notre–Dame Cathedral.

The Jacobin phase of the French Revolution unleashed a vicious ten-month Reign of Terror, during which the Committee on Public Safety, directed by Robespierre, guillotined more than seventeen thousand suspected enemies of the revolution.

French Catholics were not passive during the Reign of Terror. The most famous Catholic resistance movement occurred in the Vendee region of southwest France, from March to December 1793. The army of the Vendee marched under the banner of the Sacred Heart of Jesus and enjoyed a string of victories against the forces of the National Convention. Robespierre responded to the Vendee uprising with brutal counterforce. In August 1793, he ordered General Jean-Baptiste Carrier to employ a scorched-earth retaliation against the Vendee. From January to May 1794, the *infernales* (infernal columns) of the National Convention massacred approximately fifty thousand Vendean civilians. Among those killed were Blessed Guillaume Repin and ninety-eight other religious.

The great French writer George Bernanos memorialized the heroic resistance of sixteen Carmelite sisters who were guillotined in 1794 because they refused to renounce their religious vocations. Their crime was merely that they were religious. His book *Dialogues of the Carmelites* later served as the libretto for Francis Poulenc's 1956 opera of the same name.

Ten days after the executions of the Carmelite sisters, the moderate party of the Girondins, who had achieved a majority in the National Convention, executed Robespierre on July 28, 1794, for his ruthless campaign of terror and slaughter.

The End of the French Revolution and the Rise of Napoleon Bonaparte

On August 22, 1795, the National Convention corrected its excesses and adopted yet another French constitution establishing France's first bicameral, or two-house legislature, on the model of the US Congress's lower House of Representatives and the senatorial upper house. A five-member Directory appointed by the legislature held the power of the executive. Both Royalists and Jacobins protested the new constitution. But their objections and secret machinations to overthrow the Directory failed against the army commanded by the young and increasingly powerful Napoleon Bonaparte.

The Directory was no more successful in governing the republic of France than was the National Assembly or the National Convention. It failed to solve France's persistent financial crises, popular discontent, inefficient services, and ingrained political corruption.

The loss of public confidence in the Directory signaled an opportunity for Napoleon. On November 9, 1799, he staged a coup d'état, abolished the Directory, and appointed himself France's "first consul." Napoleon's coup marked the end of the French Revolution and the beginning of the Napoleonic era, during which France dominated most of the European continent.

The Church in France was in tatters after the French Revolution. Initially, Napoleon celebrated the collapse of the Church. But in 1800, he surprised Europe and the Church with the reestablishment of the Catholic Church. In a speech given in Milan, Napoleon said:

> I am sure that the Catholic religion is the only religion that can make a stable community happy. France has had her eyes opened through suffering, and has seen that the Catholic religion is the single anchor amid the storm. Tell the pope that I want to make him a present of thirty million Frenchmen.[11]

Napoleon's invitation to the pope is consistent with how heads of state viewed the role of the Church in a post-Westphalian world. It is for them principally a tool of the state to achieve social peace. As different as were the American and French Revolutions, both reduced Christianity to a moral system, devoid of its ordering to a transcendent reality. The Deism of the American founders and Napoleon's rapprochement with the Church both presupposed a Christianity that is a shadow of itself. They held on to certain basic concepts of Christianity, such as a Creator who ordered the universe in beneficent ways and above all Christianity's moral principles. But these attributes of Christianity were de-supernaturalized to fit the needs of the Enlightenment philosophers and statesmen. Accordingly, the moral law was stripped of its final, otherworldly ends and appropriated for civil peace.

The implications of these transformations of the Christian worldview and its principles are evident in the motto of the French Revolution: "liberty, equality, fraternity." Each of these have their origins in Christian virtues. But in the Christian moral framework, they are ordered toward supernatural ends. Consider liberty. St. Paul wrote, "When Christ freed us, he meant us to remain free" (Gal 5:1). Consider equality: in the eyes of the Lord, all are equal, whether Jew, Greek, slave, or free (Gal 3:28). And consider fraternity: our adoption as sons and daughter of God through the sacrifice of Christ makes us all brothers and sisters in Christ (Rom 8:15, 9:26; Gal 3:26).

The secularization of these virtues—liberty, equality, and fraternity—bear the marks of their Christian origins. But removed from their Christian origins and context, they mutated into the persistent conflicting "isms" of the twentieth and twenty-first centuries. Liberty became the keystone of liberalism, which kicks against any restrictions on personal freedom, self-interest, and self-expression. Equality evolved into socialism and communism, which refuses to accept any hierarchy of human values and human talents. Fraternity gradually evolved into nationalistic tribalism. Each of these mutations can be traced back to their secular versions within the Enlightenment system of values. As such they have turned out to be more tyrannical than the thinking and practices of the European *ancien régimes* they slaughtered thousands to overthrow.

Romanticism's Answer to the Enlightenment: A Return to the Fullness of Reality

The Napoleonic era ended in 1814. Forced by the Europe's Great Powers, the French deposed Napoleon and exiled him to Elba, an island off the coast of Northern Italy. The restoration of the Bourbon monarchy followed next. Napoleon escaped from Elba for one last attempt at restoring his Empire. It failed and the small island of St. Helena off the coast of West Africa became Napoleon's exilic home until his death in 1821.

The Congress of Vienna (1814–1815) reconstituted the European political order, and inaugurated a century of comparative international peace. To be sure, there were short-lived localized wars, such as the Crimean War (1853–1856), and the Franco-Prussian (1870–1871). But there was no war on a global scale until the Great War of 1914. Insurrections and revolutions, however, abounded, They were the aftershocks of the American and French Revolutions. There was the Revolution of 1832 (memorialized by Victor Hugo in *Les Misérables*, which later became a runaway success in theater and film). Followed by the Revolutions of 1848, the largest republican and democratic insurrections Europe ever faced. In America, although historians tend to see the War Between the States of 1861 as a civil war, it too was infused with a revolutionary spirit. Among some Southerners and historians, the American Civil War is known as the Second American Revolution.

Enlightenment political ideas celebrating individualism and the general disdain for inherited institutions provided the philosophical grounding for this series of European and American revolutions. Romanticism

(1790–1850), the historical period immediately following the Enlightenment carried forward Enlightenment ideals of individual freedom, the rule of nation-states against the rule of hereditary dynasties, and the spirit of rebellion. But in contrast to the Enlightenment's general disregard for history and the past, romanticism celebrated history and invented the modern discipline of history. It especially valued the European middle ages. Architects working in the romantic era designed Churches of all denominations in the Medieval Gothic Style and applied Gothic elements to government buildings and railway stations. Above all, romantic writers and poets revered Dante, recovering the *Divine Comedy* and translating into a variety of languages. Theologians and musicians set about recovering the authentic practice of Medieval chants, which in turn gave rise to a new liturgical movement in the Church.

What is romanticism? First of all, it has nothing in common with twenty-first century associations of romantic with sentimental love songs or romantic dinners by candlelight. Rather it is an artistic, philosophical, and political movement eager to explore the unfamiliar to arrive eventually back at the familiar—to home. In the romantic imagination home was associated with Ancient Rome. As G. K. Chesterton put it, "the very word 'romance' has in it the mystery and ancient meaning of Rome."[12]

Romanticism also rebelled against the Enlightenment way of seeing the world, apprehending its value mainly if not solely by a form of calculating reasoning. In this respect Romantics were at one with Vico's critique of Enlightenment thinkers who saw only madness in their rules of mathematized reasoning applied to human society and politics.

Romanticism opened up human thought and apprehension of the world to the fall range of reality, not just to that part best understood by mathematical methods of reason. In this sense, as the great historian, Jacques Barzun, wrote, "romanticism = realism."[13] By which he meant that exploring and giving expression to all of reality was the aim of romanticism.

Romantics also sought to unify the experience of the universe and re-connect what the Enlightenment had divided and isolated. The idea of referring to music, architecture, poetry, fiction, drama, painting, sculpture, and dance as "the arts" is a romantic ideal. It exemplifies the belief that apprehending the full breadth of reality is the same for all artists. They differ only in the medium in which they express their experiences—in sound, stone, paint, word, or movement.

Up Close and Personal:
EROICA: A PORTRAIT OF LUDWIG VAN BEETHOVEN (1770–1827)

Ludwig van Beethoven (1770–1827) bridged the classical and romantic periods of music. Born in the city of Bonn, located on the banks of the Rhine in what is now the German state of North Rhine-Westphalia, Beethoven has come to epitomize the tormented, temperamental artistic genius. As the heir apparent to the celebrity of Wolfgang Amadeus Mozart, he began his musical career imitating Mozart's classical style. But soon his own musical voice emerged. It was powerful, dramatic, playful, iconoclastic, and large. In many ways Beethoven's music is the soundtrack for the Napoleonic era, just as Mozart's music soundtracked the Enlightenment. His early Mozartian phase gave way in the early 1800s to a heroic style, characterized by an outpouring of music composed on a grand scale. In Beethoven's words, "I am not satisfied with the work I have done so far. From now on I intend to take a new way."[14]

Chief among his compositions in the heroic style was his Third Symphony in E-flat major, Op. 55, known as the *Eroica*, written in 1803–1804. The symphony was a musical rendering of Napoleon Bonaparte's career. An admirer of heroic revolutionary leaders, Beethoven initially titled the Third Symphony "Bonaparte." But when Napoleon declared himself emperor in 1804, Beethoven scratched out Napoleon's name from the manuscript's title page, and the symphony was published in 1806 as *Eroica* with the subtitle "In Celebration of the Memory of a Great Man." The *Eroica* symphony was longer and larger in scope than Beethoven's first two symphonies, a clear and deliberate departure from his first two symphonies in the classical, courtly style. (For a performance of Beethoven's *Eroica* symphony, see musical example 6.1 at https://www.avemariapress.com/church-and-the-age-of-enlightenment-art.)

Beethoven's association with Napoleon did not end with the Third Symphony. In 1808, Napoleon's brother, Jérôme Bonaparte, then king of Westphalia, offered Beethoven a well-paying position as kapellmeister at the court in Cassel. Jérôme's offer set off a bidding war for Beethoven's service; Archduke Rudolf, Prince Kinsky, and Prince Lobkowitz made a lucrative counter offer to Beethoven to keep him in Vienna. Beethoven accepted the offer, but events caused by the Napoleonic wars caused the offer to fall through.

In June 1813, when a coalition of forces led by the Duke of Wellington defeated Napoleon at the Battle of Vitoria, Beethoven composed a work commemorating the event. He titled it *Wellington's Victory*, Op. 91, also known as the *Battle Symphony*. He also composed music for the many events associated with the Congress of Vienna, the first pan-European conference since the conference of Westphalia in 1648. The Congress of Vienna in 1814 marked the end of the Napoleonic Wars and the beginning of a century without a global conflict. In honor of the Vienna conference, Beethoven composed the cantata *Glorious Moment* (Op. 136). (For a performance of the opening chorus of Beethoven's *Glorious Moment*, see musical example 6.2 at https://www.avemariapress.com/church-and-the-age-of-enlightenment-art.

The chorus sings, "Europe stands! And the times that ever move forward, the chorus of peoples and the old centuries look on in wonder. Who must that noble figure be, that clad in the wonderful brilliance of the old world of the gods ascends from the east in princely majesty on to the rainbow of peace? Many delighted people stand, calling to the glorious figure adorned with crowns girt with light: Stand and stay! Give the great crowds of people counsel and news in answer to them.")

But perhaps Beethoven's most enduring contribution to the Enlightenment ethos was his Ninth Symphony (Op. 125), which featured a full chorus in its fourth movement. Composed between 1822 and 1824, it was first performed in Vienna on May 7, 1824. The symphony is a towering achievement in the history of music and perhaps one of the most popular works in the orchestral repertory. It continues to be the most performed symphony in the world. The choral text is the "Ode to Joy," written by Friedrich Schiller in 1785 and revised in 1803, with text additions made by Beethoven. Its aspiration that "All men will become brothers," overcoming the differences of custom and ethnicity, echoes the social aims of the Enlightenment and has become an anthem for freedom. Chinese students played recordings of it during the 1989 Tiananmen Square protests. Leonard Bernstein conducted a performance of it on Christmas Day 1989, following the fall of the Berlin Wall, replacing the word *joy* with *freedom*. (For a performance of the Fourth Movement of Beethoven's Ninth Symphony, which includes the "Ode to Joy," see musical example 6.3 at https://www.avemariapress.com/church-and-the-age-of-enlightenment-art. This is the performance conducted by Leonard Bernstein celebrating German reunification in 1989.)

St. John Henry Newman

No other great figure of the nineteenth century felt the desire for reuniting what had been divided by the Enlightenment more than St. John Henry Newman. His life spanned nearly the entire nineteenth century, from 1801 to 1890. Although his writings cannot be contained by the category of romanticism, he shares much in common with significant elements of the Romantics' project: the importance of history as a meaningful source of knowledge, the unity of all truth, the reintegration of the human mind with the totality of what it means to think and know the world, and intellectual restlessness together with a fervent desire for a true home, which for him was Rome—the Roman Catholic Church.

Newman was born in London on February 21, 1801, the eldest of six children born to John and Jemima Newman. Newman's father was a banker, and Jemima Newman descended from a notable family of Huguenot refugees in England. At seven years of age, Newman attended Great Ealing School. He was a serious student, little involved in sports or extracurricular activities. He read voraciously, especially the novels of Walter Scott and Robert Southey.

When he was fourteen he read Enlightenment thinkers, such as Thomas Paine, David Hume, John Locke, and Voltaire. Unnerved by Enlightenment skepticism and irreligion, he converted at fifteen to Evangelical Christianity and immersed himself in the English Calvinist tradition. Newman described it as a religion of personal prayer and Bible reading, with an extreme antipathy to Roman Catholicism. Later in his life, he looked back on his conversion to Evangelical Christianity as the saving of his soul. Nevertheless, he gradually moved away from Evangelicalism. As one of his biographers wrote, "[Newman] came to see Evangelicalism, with its emphasis on religious feeling and on the Reformation doctrine of justification by faith alone, as a Trojan horse for an undogmatic religious individualism that ignored the Church's role in the

transmission of revealed truth, and that must lead inexorably to subjec-
tivism and skepticism."[15]

English Evangelicalism combined seventeenth-century Puritanism,
eighteenth-century Methodism, and elements of Lutheran pietism. Its
influence was pervasive, and its social effects were significant. It was,
for instance, the driving force behind the abolition of the slave trade. Its
dour seriousness, its belief in the unregenerate evil of human nature, and
a gradual narrowing of its intellectual outlook made Evangelicalism the
target of acerbic characterizations in the great Victorian novelists, such
as Anthony Trollope. At Oxford, Cambridge, and other English universities, Evangelicals were despised and occupied the lowest rung in their
social systems.

In 1817 Newman entered Trinity College, Oxford. His anxiety to do
well in his final exams overwhelmed him such that he broke down in the
examination and barely qualified to take the bachelor of arts. Following
his graduation from Trinity, he won a fellowship at Oriel College, Oxford.
Newman held fast to his Evangelical creed during his years at Trinity and
Oriel. Oriel's provost remembered Newman as a serious and shy student,
who kept to himself amid an Oxford that at that time celebrated vigorous
debate and boisterous argument.

The silence of Newman struck the provost of Oriel College as surpris-
ing and unexpected. This remark calls to mind the taunt of "Dumb Ox"
directed at St. Thomas Aquinas by his classmates. Yet, Thomas's teacher,
St. Albert the Great, prophesied to the students, "You call this man a
dumb ox, but his bellowing in doctrine will one day resound throughout
the world."[16] One can say the same of Newman.

Newman's second spiritual awakening occurred in 1826, when he
fell under the influence of Richard Whatley, one of the most original and
formidable of the great Oxford professors. Whatley was equally hostile
to high church Anglicanism and Newman's middle-class Evangelicalism. He was a leader of the Oriel school of Anglican liberalism. Despite

Whatley's harsh views on Evangelicalism, Newman became devoted to Whately, and Whatley relished the idea of turning the young Newman to the cause of liberalism.

No one could have predicted that Newman would become one of the nineteenth century's staunchest critics of liberalism. Under the influence of another Oxford figure, Hurrell Froude, Newman began to see that liberalism was unimaginative and intellectually shallow, and the greatest danger to Christianity. When Pope Leo XIII made Newman a cardinal in 1879, Newman gave his famous Biglietto Speech (named after the formal letter given to cardinals on such occasions). The speech is a systematic indictment of liberalism, which he called the "one great mischief" against which he had set his face "from the first."[17]

Chief among the liberal ideas that Newman "denounced and abjured" were those originating in Enlightenment thought. He pushed back against the Enlightenment-based liberal idea that "no theological doctrine is anything more than an opinion which happens to be held by bodies of men." Such a position, said Newman, nullified the reality of divine revelation. An associated Enlightenment idea—"no one can believe what he does not understand"—reversed the time-honored principle that faith comes before understanding (*fides quaerens intellectum*).

Newman especially set himself against the Enlightenment's precept that "no revealed doctrines or precepts may reasonably stand in the way of scientific conclusions." This way of thinking was prevalent among Enlighteners and even among Christian writers influenced by them. Such writers wrote innumerable books compiling evidence for the reasonableness of Christianity. In so doing they ceded too much to the Enlightenment and did violence to the boundless mystery of God.

Newman rejected this approach to Christian belief for its cold aloofness to the warmth of a loving fatherly God. He could not reconcile faith in the living God with a businesslike calculation, the heaping up of evidence, and the exercise of mind alone. Rather, faith was a movement of the deepest longings of the human heart. Newman was of one mind with the great romantic poet Samuel Taylor Coleridge when he wrote, "Evidences of Christianity! I am weary of the word. Make a man feel the want of it; rouse him, if you can, to the self-knowledge of his need of it; and you may safely trust it to its own Evidence."[18]

Newman was above all a unifier, exhibiting everywhere in his writings and sermons an integrative and synthesizing habit of mind. Wherever he turned, Newman saw the reign of disunity, especially in the Church and in social life. His first effort was directed at the pressing need to reintegrate faith and reason. In a series of sermons given at the University of Oxford between 1839 and 1841, Newman vehemently rejected the Enlightenment's opposition of faith and reason. He refused to concede that only the natural sciences had any claims on truth and that religious statements carried only emotional significance. For Newman, both faith and reason were sources of knowledge and action. Disuniting them severely limited authentic human flourishing.

Newman enlarged the scope of how humans reason by reuniting intellect with the heart and experience. Drawing on his own experience of conversion to Roman Catholicism, at one point he seemed convinced by the evidence of his research that the Roman Catholic Church was the true Church founded by Jesus Christ and the apostles. A friend asked him why he delayed his conversion. Newman replied that it is not enough to be moved to action by intellect alone, for the "whole man moves . . . all the logic in the world would not have made me move faster toward Rome than I did."[19]

For Newman, the Enlightenment view of the thinking person as a calculator, who weighs up evidence for and against an argument with no personal investment in the outcome, had no basis in human nature as it really is. No person, said Newman, will be a martyr for a conclusion reached by such cold reasoning. A person "is not a reasoning animal; he is a seeing, feeling, contemplating, acting animal."[20] He or she is moved not by mind alone but by the heart, which, like Pascal, Newman sees as the essence of the human person and the seat of mere feeling. "The heart," wrote Newman, "is commonly reached, not through the reason [alone], but through the imagination, by means of direct impressions, by the testimony of facts and events, by history, by description. Persons influence us, voices melt us, looks subdue us, deeds inflame us."[21]

Newman did not celebrate the triumph of heart over head, emotions over intellect. Rather, he proposed a more realistic model of how persons actually arrive at a conclusion that would shape their commitments and ways of living. Instead of the simplistic Enlightenment view of rationality, he described the complex ways in which human beings actually arrive at their core convictions, in science and daily life, and their religious beliefs.

During the course of his long life, Newman tackled nearly every religious and societal problem and issue that can be traced back in some way to the Enlightenment project. Many of these problems and issues persist to the twenty-first century. Thus, Newman is considered a saint for our times and a profound influence on the fathers of the Second Vatican Council (1962–1965). Pope Benedict acknowledged the root of the council's universal call to holiness in Newman's way of life. "Newman," said Pope Benedict, "tells us that our divine Master has assigned a specific task to each one of us, a 'definite service,' committed uniquely to every single person: 'I have my mission', he wrote, 'I am a link in a chain, a bond of connexion between persons. He has not created me for naught. I shall do good, I shall do his work; I shall be an angel of peace, a preacher of truth in my own place . . . if I do but keep his commandments and serve him in my calling.'"[22]

Great Britain somehow avoided the revolutions that spasmed continental Europe, culminating in waves of insurrection during 1848. But for Newman, the 1840s was a decade of great internal tumult as he sought mightily to discern whether to convert to Roman Catholicism. In 1843, Newman began writing perhaps his most influential book, *An Essay on the Development of Christian Doctrine.* He wrote the book as not an objective, arms-length historical study but rather a high-stakes personal undertaking—a matter of weighty consequence for his continued membership in the Church of England, and thereby the life he enjoyed as an Oxford don. When he undertook the writing of the *Essay*, his mind was set that he would act in accord with the findings of the *Essay*. His will would follow his intellect.

His discovery in 1845 that the doctrine of the Roman Catholic Church had the rightful claim to be continuous with the revelation of Jesus Christ to his apostles and, through them, to all humankind led him to seek reception into the Church of Rome in the same year of the *Essay*'s first publication. In the postscript to the 1845 edition of the *Essay*, Newman wrote:

> Since the [*Essay on the Development of Christian Doctrine*] was written, the Author [Newman] has joined the Catholic Church. It was his intention and wish to have carried his Volume through the Press before deciding finally on this step. But when he had got some way in the printing, he recognized in himself a conviction of the truth of the conclusion to which the discussion leads, so clear as to supersede further deliberation. Shortly afterwards circumstances gave him the opportunity of acting upon it, and he felt that he had no warrant for refusing to do so.[23]

Newman presented himself for instruction in the Catholic faith to Fr. Dominic Barberi, a Passionist priest living in London at that time. In October 1845, Newman made his confession to Fr. Barberi. In his *Apologia Pro Vita Sua*, published in 1864, Newman recalled how Fr. Barberi arrived at his apartment "soaked from the rain and . . . drying himself by the fire" when Newman knelt and asked to be received into the Catholic Church.[24] This event is marked by a sculpture in the Catholic Church of Blessed Dominic Barberi at Littlemore, England.

Although many admire Newman for his keen intellect by which he challenged and corrected many of the Enlightenment's mistaken ideas about human life, he also lived a unity of life that witnessed against the

Enlightenment's empire of division. Pope Benedict underscored this aspect of Newman's life.

> While it is John Henry Newman's intellectual legacy that has understandably received most attention in the vast literature devoted to his life and work, I prefer on this occasion to conclude with a brief reflection on his life as a priest, a pastor of souls. The warmth and humanity underlying his appreciation of the pastoral ministry is beautifully expressed in another of his famous sermons: "Had Angels been your priests, my brethren, they could not have condoled with you, sympathized with you, have had compassion on you, felt tenderly for you, and made allowances for you, as we can; they could not have been your patterns and guides, and have led you on from your old selves into a new life, as they can who come from the midst of you."[25]

When Newman converted to Roman Catholicism he was forced to leave a life of high prestige as a celebrated Oxford professor and Anglican theologian. He found greater joy in an apostolate devoted to the care for the people of Birmingham, a city that was ravaged by another revolution—the industrial revolution that brought with it great benefits to humankind, but also great misery and upheavals to those at the lower ranks of society. To these, the new urban poor, Newman lavished great care and consolation.

YOU BE THE JUDGE:

Was the American Revolution an enlightened or a conservative revolution?

It is commonplace to view the American Revolution of 1776 as the first large-scale realization of the political principles of the Enlightenment. The American Revolution and the Constitutional

Convention of 1787 in Philadelphia were important to many Europeans and Americans because they demonstrated that Enlightenment ideals could indeed be put into practice. Americans threw off the shackles of monarchical rule and created a new nation by a Declaration of Independence that adopted John Locke's political principles in arguing that government is instituted by the people in a contract to protect their lives, liberties, and property and that they can revoke that contract when a government fails in those responsibilities.

Americans also followed Locke in 1787 by instituting a new contract: the United States Constitution. They were strongly influenced by the French Enlightenment political philosopher Baron de Montesquieu (1689–1755) in establishing a government separating and balancing its powers among three branches: the executive, the legislative, and the judiciary. They realized Voltaire's ideas of the necessity of guaranteeing individuals' freedom of expression and religion and refusing to establish a state church. They followed Rousseau in establishing a wide franchise (adult, propertied, free males) and reserving political power to more localized communities (states). They perhaps also followed an implication of Rousseau's thought in allowing the majority white population to declare Black slaves three-fifths of a person.

But there is another way to view the American Revolution other than its apparent adoption of Enlightenment principles. A political revolution is the violent transfer of power and property for the sake of an idea. The American Revolution certainly fits this description of a revolution. But it can also be seen by the light of another meaning of revolution, that is, a revolving, as when the Earth makes one revolution around the sun each year. In this meaning of revolution there is a circling that returns to an original position.

This idea of revolution of return was more in character with Americans who fought a war to conserve what they believed to be their ancient rights as Englishmen. It also resonates in unison with one of two major speeches that Edmund Burke made in the

English House of Commons at the start of the American War for Independence, "Conciliation with the Colonies" (1775). The Americans, he said, are not devoted to liberty in the abstract, such as we would find among the Enlightenment *philosophes*, "but to Liberty according to English ideas, and on English principles. Abstract Liberty, like other mere abstractions, is not to be found."[26]

Burke insisted that Americans' commitment to freedom did not disqualify them as subjects of the English monarchy. In fact, Burke underscored the political kinship between the American colonists and their English cousins. In Burke's analysis, the colonists in 1775 were not enthusiastic to establish a republic government. They were driven to that political outcome because of the shortsightedness and arbitrary conduct of England's ministers, who had abandoned their role as guardians of social well-being. The preservation of freedom, once a joint responsibility of the mother country and its colonists, in Burke's view, had passed to the responsibility of the Americans. In this sense, the American Revolution was a conservative undertaking—the preservation of long-standing inherited liberties.

Conclusion

This history of the Enlightenment began with Europe's first Great War—the Thirty Years' War—and ended with another European war—the Napoleonic Wars. The horrors of the first war prompted a total rethinking of European religious and political practices. Indeed, it prompted a rethinking of thinking itself and the trustworthiness of inherited patterns of thought in order to avoid such wars in the future. The second war, in large part, was the product of this rethinking. Napoleon's armies were the missionaries of Enlightenment and revolutionary ideas.

So what gains were made? To find out, we need to look beyond the surface of events to the core of the Enlightenment project. Revolutions such as those wrought by the Enlightenment are indices of spiritual discontent and change. The American and French Revolutions were not so much protests against misgovernment and oppressive practices as they were efforts to remake the Euro-American social order on the foundation of new ideas. The revolutionaries did not limit themselves to political reforms such as drafting new constitutions and establishing new legal codes; rather, they aspired to refashion society from its roots. The new calendar introduced by the Jacobins, for example, signified a total break with the past and the conviction that a new era had dawned for humanity.

To be sure, excesses of the French Revolution, most notably the Reign of Terror, were reined in by subsequent regimes. But the mere fact that it occurred at all should have called into question the Enlightenment's extravagant optimism in the progress of human affairs based on human reason. For the French Revolution was the laboratory for Enlightenment thinking. But amazingly the Enlightenment's faith in progress persisted and continues to persist into the twenty-first century. Its staying power rests not so much on its ideas, which have been challenged, and in some cases defeated, by post-Enlightenment secular thinkers and political actors. The idea of progress in human affairs continues to find adherents because technology keeps delivering on the Enlightenment goal of making life materially better for more and more people. The devastation of two world wars in the twentieth century, the development of weapons of mass destruction, and much else that points to moral and human regress, and not progress, are insufficient to defeat Europeans' and Americans' faith in progress.

The cult of technologically driven human progress proceeds from the victory of the Enlightenment's narrowing of human reason to mathematized, calculating reason. Even though questions about the ultimate things that really matter to men and women cannot be answered satisfactorily by calculating reason, the Enlightenment bracketed these questions and set them aside on the grounds that we have or cannot get definite answers to them. They have thus been cast away from serious consideration in the public realm and left to the private realm of personal preference. Still, the human heart—and I am now speaking of the Pascalian meaning of heart—longs for answers and a public life supportive of living a common life in accord with the heart's deepest longings. Technology cannot respond to these longings, but it can distract us from seeking their true satisfaction.

Notes

1. The Thirty Years' War and Its Aftermath

1. Peter Hamish Wilson, *The Holy Roman Empire, 1495–1806* (New York: MacMillan Press, 1999), 2; Erik von Kuehnelt-Leddihn, *The Menace of the Herd or Procrustes at Large* (Milwaukee: Bruce Publishing, 1943), 164.

2. Quoted in Warren H. Carroll, *The Cleaving of Christendom* (Front Royal, VA: Christendom Press, 2000), 510.

3. Stephen M. Barr, *Modern Physics and Ancient Faith* (Notre Dame, IN: University of Notre Dame Press, 2003); I. Bernard Cohen, *Revolution in Science* (Cambridge, MA: Harvard University Press, 1985); Ronald L. Numbers, *Galileo Goes to Jail and Other Myths about Science and Religion* (Cambridge, MA: Harvard University Press, 2010).

4. This incident is a slightly fictionalized account of an actual event collected in Volkmar Happe, *Thuringian Chronicle*, ed. Hans Medick, Norbert Winnige, and Andreas Bahr (Jena, Germany: Thüringer Universitäts und Landesbibliothek Jena, 2008).

5. From Peter Hagendorf, *Diary of a Mercenary from the Thirty Years War*, ed. Jan Peters, 2nd rev. ed. (Göttingen, Germany: V & R Unipress, 2012), 127, 128.

6. This account draws on several historical documents collected in Maurus Friesenegger, *Diary from the Thirty Years War: From a Manuscript in the Andechs Cloister*, ed. Willibald Mathaser (Munich, Germany: Allitera Verlag, 2007), 17–18.

7. "Two Noteworthy Documents from the Time of the Swedish War in the Winter of 1634–1635, regarding the Terrible Hunger in Agawang," in *Annual Report of the District Historical Association for the Administrative Region of Swabia and Neuburg*, ed. Franz von Baader (Augsburg, Germany: Hartmannsche Buchdruckerei, 1872), 71–72.

8. This story is a slightly fictionalized account of an actual event described in Martin Botzinger, "Vitae Curriculo," in *Contributions to the Explanation of the History of the Princely Saxon-Hildburghausen Church, School, and Land, part 1, Creitz*, ed. Johann Werner Kraus, 349–68 (Greiz, Germany: Abraham Gottlieb Ludewig, 1750), 353–56.

9. Saul S. Friedman, *The Oberammergau Passion Play* (Carbondale, IL: Southern Illinois University Press, 1984).

10. Vincent de Paul, *Correspondence, Conferences, Documents* (Brooklyn, NY: New City Press, 1985).

11. De Paul, *Correspondence, Conferences, Documents*.

2. What Is the Enlightenment?

1. Stephen Gaukroger, *Francis Bacon and the Transformation of Early-Modern Philosophy* (New York: Cambridge University Press, 2001), 86.

2. Denis De Lucca, "The Dissemination of Jesuit Military Mathematics from the Collegio Romano to the Emilia-Romagna Region of Italy, 1600–1750," *Journal of Baroque Studies* 1, no. 1 (2013): 78.

3. Jean-Pierre de Caussade, *Self-Abandonment to Divine Providence* (Charlotte, NC: Tan Books, 2012), x.

4. Caussade, *Self-Abandonment*, 23.

5. Caussade, *Self-Abandonment*, xi.

6. Caussade, *Self-Abandonment*, 11.

7. Caussade, *Self-Abandonment*, 31.

8. Caussade, *Self-Abandonment*, 15.

9. Quoted in Gabriel R. Ricci, *Politics in Religion: Religion in Public Life* (New York: Taylor & Francis, 2017), 4.

10. Christopher Dawson, *Progress and Religion* (Peru, IL: Sherwood Sugdon & Company, 1991), 192.

11. Quoted in Peter Gay, ed., *The Enlightenment: A Compendium* (New York: Simon & Schuster, 1973), 64.

12. Quoted in Gay, *Enlightenment*.

13. Edward Dolnick, *The Clockwork Universe: Isaac Newton, the Royal Society, and the Birth of the Modern World* (New York: Harper, 2012).

14. Gay, *Enlightenment*, 69–70.

15. Gay, *Enlightenment*, 388.

16. Gay, *Enlightenment*, 388.

17. Gay, *Enlightenment*, 585.

18. Gay, *Enlightenment*, 585.

19. Gay, *Enlightenment*, 602.

20. Thomas Paine, *Common Sense: The Origin and Design of Government* (Dublin, OH: Coventry House Publishing, 2016), 72.

21. Thomas Paine, *Age of Reason* (Grand Rapids, MI: Michigan Legal Publishing, 2014), 3.

22. David Brewster, *Memoirs of the Life, Writings, and Discoveries of Sir Isaac Newton* (London: Thomas Constable, 1855), 407.

23. Caussade, *Self-Abandonment*, 30.

24. Caussade, *Self-Abandonment*, 30.

25. Francis de Sales, *Treatise on the Love of God* (London: Aeterna Press, 2015), 101–2.

3. The Religious Enlightenment

1. Blaise Pascal, *Pensees*, trans. W. F. Trotter (Overland Park, KS: Digireads.com Publishing, 2018), 56.

2. Blaise Pascal, *Great Shorter Works of Pascal*, trans. Emile Cailliet and John C. Blankenagel (Philadelphia: Westminster Press, 1948), 117.

3. David Sorkin, *The Religious Enlightenment: Protestants, Jews, and Catholics from London to Vienna* (Princeton, NJ: Princeton University Press, 2008), 167.

4. Sorkin, *Religious Enlightenment*, 180.

5. Sorkin, *Religious Enlightenment*, 185.

6. Sorkin, *Religious Enlightenment*, 232

7. Sorkin, *Religious Enlightenment*, 232.

8. Sorkin, *Religious Enlightenment*, 230.

9. Sorkin, *Religious Enlightenment*, 234.

10. Sorkin, *Religious Enlightenment*, 240.

11. Sorkin, *Religious Enlightenment*, 237.

12. Anonymous, *Saint Gertrude the Great: The Herald of Divine Love* (Charlotte, NC: Tan Books, 2014), 27–29.

13. Emile Bougaud, *Life of Blessed Margaret Mary Alacoque* (New York: Benzinger Brothers, 1890), 164.

14. Bougaud, *Life of Blessed Margaret Mary Alacoque*, 176.

15. Romano Guardini, *The Lord* (Washington, DC: Regnery Publishers, 1954), 485–87.

16. Pascal, *Pensees*, 66.

4. The Enlightenment in the Tradition of European Renewal Movements

1. Christopher Dawson, *Progress and Religion* (Peru, IL: Sherwood Sugden, 1991), 27.

2. Quoted in Christopher Dawson, *Religion and the Rise of Western Culture* (New York: Image Books, 1958), 65.

3. Daniel Kennedy, "St. Albertus Magnus," in *The Catholic Encyclopedia*, vol. 1 (New York: Robert Appleton, 1907), accessed May 6, 2022, https://www.newadvent.org/cathen/01264a.htm.

4. Quoted in Jacques Barzun, *From Dawn to Decadence: 500 Years of Western Cultural Life* (New York: Harper Collins, 2000), 5.

5. Quoted in Barzun, *From Dawn to Decadence*, 7.

6. Augustine of Hippo, *Sermons*, vol. 10, trans. Edmund Hill (Hyde Park, NY: New City Press, 1997), sermon 336, 1 (PL 38, 1472).

7. Augustine of Hippo, *Confessions*, trans. J. G. Pilkington (New York: Heritage Press, 1963), 141.

8. Quoted in Karol Berger, *Bach's Cycle, Mozart's Arrow: An Essay on the Origins of Musical Modernity* (Berkeley: University of California Press, 2007), 128.

9. Quoted in Barzun, *From Dawn to Decadence*, 209.

10. Joseph Gelinueau, *The Psalms: A New Translation* (New York: Paulist Press, 1963), 180.

5. The New Politics of the Enlightenment

1. Innocent X, *Zelo Domus Dei*, in *Readings in Church History*, ed. Colman J. Barry, 715–18 (Westminster, MD: Christian Classics, 1960).

2. John Locke, "An Essay concerning the True Original Extent and End of Civil Government," in *Social Contract*, ed. Ernest Barker (New York: Oxford University Press, 1960), 29.

3. Thomas Hobbes, *Leviathan* (New York: Norton, 2020), 89–90.

4. Hobbes, *Leviathan*, 118.

5. Hobbes. *Leviathan*, 15.

6. Hobbes, *Leviathan*, 144–45.

7. Giambattista Vico, *New Science* (New York: Penguin Books, 1999), 479.

8. Giambattista Vico, *On the Most Ancient Wisdom of the Italians* (Ithaca, NY: Cornell University Press, 1988), 98–99.

9. Nicholas de Condorcet, *Outlines of an Historical View of the Progress of the Human Mind* (Philadelphia: M. Carey, 1795), 12, https://oll.libertyfund.org/title/condorcet-outlines-of-an-historical-view-of-the-progress-of-the-human-mind.

10. Quoted in Benedict XVI, "General Audience: Saint Alphonsus Liguori," March 30, 2011, Holy See, accessed June 26, 2022, https://www.vatican.va/content/benedict-xvi/en/audiences/2011/documents/hf_ben-xvi_aud_20110330.html.

11. Alasdair MacIntyre, *Dependent Rational Animals: Why Human Beings Need the Virtues* (Chicago: Open Court Publishing, 1999), 5.

12. O. Carter Snead, *What It Means to Be Human* (Cambridge, MA: Harvard University Press), 98.

13. Alphonsus de Liguori, *Duties and Dignities of the Priest*, ed. Eugene Grimm (Brooklyn, NY: Redemptorist Fathers, 1927), 217.

14. Office for the Liturgical Celebrations of the Supreme Pontiff, "Liturgical Vestments and the Vesting Prayers," Holy See, accessed May 6, 2022, https://www.vatican.va/news_services/liturgy/details/ns_lit_doc_20100216_vestizione_en.html.

15. William Weber, "Handel's London: Political, Social and Intellectual Contexts," in *Cambridge Companion to Handel*, ed. Donald Burrows (New York: Cambridge University Press, 1997), 53.

16. Quoted in Elaine R. Sissman, "Learned Style and Rhetoric of the Sublime in the 'Jupiter' Symphony," in *Wolfgang Amadè Mozart: Essays on his Life and Music*, ed. Stanley Sadie, 213–40 (Oxford, UK: Clarendon Press, 1996).

6. The Enlightenment in Action: The American and French Revolutions

1. Weber, "Handel's London," 52.

2. Edmund Burke, *Reflections on the Revolution in France* (New York: Penguin Books, 1968), 153.

3. Felipe Fernandez-Armesto, *1492: The Year the World Began* (New York: HarperCollins, 2009), 2.

4. Quoted in James R. Leek, *The Evangelization of the New World: Hispanic Influence in American History* (Fort Scott, KS: St. Paul's Publishing, 1987), 41–42.

5. James Otis, "1763: Otis, Rights of British Colonies Asserted," Online Library of Liberty, accessed April 9, 2021, https://oll.libertyfund.org/pages/1763-otis-rights-of-british-colonies-asserted-pamphlet.

6. "Declaration of Independence: A Transcription," National Archives, accessed April 9, 2021, https://www.archives.gov/founding-docs/declaration-transcript.

7. "Jefferson's 'Original Rough Draught' of the Declaration of Independence," The Papers of Thomas Jefferson, accessed April 9, 2021, https://jeffersonpapers.princeton.edu/selected-documents/jefferson%E2%80%99s-%E2%80%9C-original-rough-draught%E2%80%9D-declaration-independence.

8. Francis, "Homily of His Holiness Pope Francis, May 2, 2015," Homilies of Pope Francis, accessed April 9, 2021, http://www.vatican.va/content/francesco/en/homilies/2015/documents/papa-francesco_20150502_omelia-pontifical-north-american-college.html.

9. "Declaration of the Rights of Man—1789," Avalon Project: Documents in Law, History and Diplomacy, 2008, https://avalon.law.yale.edu/18th_century/rightsof.asp.

10. "The Constitution of 1791 National Assembly, September 3, 1791," Internet Archive, accessed April 9, 2021, https://web.archive.org/web/20111217062556/http://sourcebook.fsc.edu/history/constitutionof1791.html#expand.

11. Eamon Duffy, *Saints and Sinners: A History of the Popes* (New Haven, CT: Yale University Press, 2015), 262.

12. G. K. Chesterton, *Orthodoxy* (San Francisco: Ignatius Press, 1995), 14.

13. Jacques Barzun, *Classic, Romantic, and Modern* (Chicago: University of Chicago Press, 1961), 58.

14. Quoted in Barry Cooper, *Beethoven* (New York: Oxford University Press, 2000), 131.

15. Eamon Duffy, *John Henry Newman: A Very Brief History* (London: Society for Promoting Christian Knowledge, 2019), 25–26.

16. G. K. Chesterton, *St. Thomas Aquinas and St. Francis of Assisi in One Volume* (San Francisco: Ignatius Press, 2002), 67.

17. John Henry Newman, "Biglietto Speech," Newman Reader, accessed May 5, 2022, https://www.newmanreader.org/works/addresses/file2.html.

18. Quoted in Duffy, *John Henry Newman*, 62.

19. John Henry Newman, *Apologia Pro Vita Sua* (New York: Norton, 1968), 136.

20. John Henry Newman, *An Essay in Aid of a Grammar of Assent* (Oxford: Oxford University Press, 1985), 76.

21. Quoted in Duffy, *John Henry Newman*, 63.

22. Benedict XVI, "Mass with the Beatification of Venerable Cardinal John Henry Newman," September 19, 2010, Holy See, accessed May 6, 2022, https://www.vatican.va/content/benedict-xvi/en/homilies/2010/documents/hf_ben-xvi_hom_20100919_beatif-newman.html.

23. Newman, *An Essay on the Development of Christian Doctrine* (Notre Dame, IN: University of Notre Dame Press, 1989), x–xi.

24. Newman, *Apologia*, 181–82.

25. Benedict XVI, "Mass with the Beatification of Venerable Cardinal John Henry Newman."

26. Edmund Burke, *Pre-Revolutionary Writings*, ed. Ian Harris (New York: Cambridge University Press, 1993), 222.

Index

187

Dominic A. Aquila is professor of history and director of institutional effectiveness and assessment at the University of St. Thomas in Houston, Texas, where he was founding dean of the School of Arts and Sciences and served as provost and vice president for academic affairs and dean of graduate studies. Aquila was professor of history and founding dean of the School of Liberal Arts at the University of Saint Francis in Fort Wayne, Indiana. He also taught at a number of other colleges and universities, including Franciscan University of Steubenville, the University of Rochester, and Rochester Institute of Technology.

Aquila has doctorate degrees in higher education administration from Texas Tech University and in history from the University of South Africa. He earned an advanced degree in history from the University of Rochester. Aquila has an MBA from New York University and a bachelor's degree in music from the Julliard School. He also did graduate studies in composition at the Eastman School of Music. Aquila has published a number of scholarly and popular articles in the *Catholic Social Science Review, Image: A Journal of Religion and the Arts, Our Sunday Visitor, Religions,* and *Social Justice Review.* He is involved in many professional organizations related to higher education and has received many awards for his work. He served as consultant and mentor to organizations competing in Our Sunday Visitor Foundation's 2021 Challenge for Catholic Innovators.

Aquila and his wife, Diane, have eleven children and eight grandchildren. They live in Houston.

www.stthom.edu
Facebook: dominic.aquila.733
Twitter: @DominicAAquila1
Instagram: @dominic.aquila

The Reclaiming
CATHOLIC HISTORY SERIES

The history of the Catholic Church is often clouded by myth, misinformation, and missing pieces. Today there is a renewed interest in recovering the true history of the Church, correcting the record in the wake of centuries of half-truths and noble lies. Books in the Reclaiming Catholic History series, edited by Mike Aquilina and written by leading authors and historians, bring Church history to life, debunking the myths one era at a time.

Titles in the Series Include:

The Early Church

The Church and the Roman Empire

The Church and the Dark Ages

The Church and the Middle Ages

The Church and the Age of Reformations

The Church and the Age of Enlightenment

The Church and the Modern Era